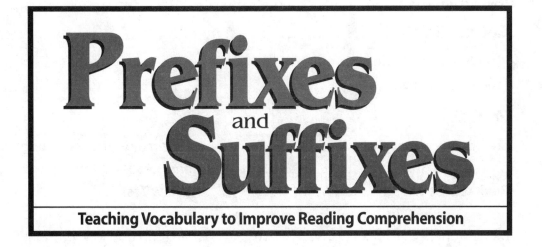

Prefixes and Suffixes

Teaching Vocabulary to Improve Reading Comprehension

Written by
Trisha Callella

Editors: Teri L. Applebaum and Sheri Rous

Cover Illustrator: Barbara Peterson

Designer/Production: Barbara Peterson/Carmela Murray

Cover Designer: Barbara Peterson

Art Director: Tom Cochrane

Project Director: Carolea Williams

Table of Contents

Introduction

Many students are good "decoders"—they know how to read a word by sounding out its parts. But often their comprehension of the word's meaning isn't as strong. All of the research in the area of comprehension agrees that a strong vocabulary is the foundation for reading comprehension. In fact, vocabulary is the foundation of all areas of literacy—listening, speaking, reading, and writing.

Since increasing and developing a student's vocabulary will improve his or her overall reading comprehension, research recommends teaching students the parts of words. Beginning at grade three, the national standards require that students use their knowledge of prefixes and suffixes to determine the meaning of words, and that they use their knowledge of root words to determine the meaning of unknown words within a passage. All words are made up of prefixes, roots, and/or suffixes. They are the meaningful chunks in every word a student reads. Too often, students skip words they don't know as they are reading. This breaks down their understanding of the text. For this reason, students need to learn how to break down the meaningful parts of unknown words so they won't skip them. This is especially important for multisyllabic words. By teaching your students how to "dissect" words using the lessons in *Prefixes and Suffixes,* they will learn how to comprehend multisyllabic words, not just decode them.

The activities in this resource incorporate all levels of literacy to maximize the transfer of vocabulary into your students' speech, writing, and reading comprehension.

Each lesson has four activity pages to teach students new vocabulary and thereby improve their comprehension skills:

- A take-home **Word List** with parts of speech to study.
- A set of hands-on **Vocabulary Sort cards** to match up for independent practice.
- A set of **Read-Around Review game cards** for small-group review and transfer of what was learned. (The definitions are rewritten in this game, so students have to think and apply what they have learned about the meanings of words. This game combines listening, speaking, and reading.)
- A **Vocabulary Quiz** using test-prep and fill-in-the blank formats that require thinking, reading, and writing. The questions extend students' learning.

Getting Started

Planning and Scheduling

The most important thing to remember when learning anything is review. Ideally, your students will overlearn these prefixes and suffixes, so that they become second nature to them. Your students will become increasingly more confident in their ability to understand larger words as they become more comfortable with "dissecting" words and defining the parts of words. The best part is that students will start using the vocabulary words you teach in their oral language and in their writing! The key is incorporating ongoing review activities and games into your everyday curriculum.

Adopt the motto "New, New, Review" in your classroom. This motto is so key to the success of building vocabulary that will transfer to all areas of literacy that this book is arranged in this exact format. For every two prefixes or suffixes, there is a review test. This serves as an easy way for you to remember that ongoing review opportunities are critical to the transfer of learning.

Teach one prefix or suffix each week, which will lead to a three-week teaching cycle. For example, you would teach a new prefix week 1, a new prefix week 2, and review the two prefixes during week 3. The review tests included in this book for each pair of prefixes or suffixes will make this schedule easy to follow. Read the information on pages 5 and 6 for directions on how to implement each lesson. Use the following Suggested Weekly Plan to help you organize and plan your teaching of prefixes and suffixes and new vocabulary.

Suggested Weekly Plan

Day 1: **Introduce vocabulary** in a pocket chart.
Pass out **Word Lists** for students to take home.
Play a **game** with the new words (see page 6).

Day 2: **Review vocabulary** in the pocket chart.
Play **Vocabulary Sort.**

Day 3: **Review vocabulary** in the pocket chart.
Play a **game** with the vocabulary words (see page 6).
Use the **Read-Around Review game cards** with small groups.

Day 4: **Review vocabulary** in the pocket chart.
Play a **game** with the vocabulary words (see page 6).
Use the **Read-Around Review game cards** with small groups.
Have **students make up questions** they think will be on the vocabulary quiz.

Day 5: **Review vocabulary** in the pocket chart.
Play a **game** with the vocabulary words (see page 6).
Have students take the **Vocabulary Quiz.**

Teaching a Lesson

Word List (Days 1–5)

Each lesson begins with a word list of ten vocabulary words that contain the prefix or suffix that is the focus for the lesson. Each list includes the part of speech and the definition for each word. Send these lists home for students to practice reading with their family.

- Introduce, teach, and review each set of vocabulary words by typing each word in a large font size and printing it on a piece of construction paper (quarter sheet of 12" x 18" or 30.5 cm x 46 cm construction paper). Do the same for each definition. Display these enlarged word cards in a large pocket chart for hands-on manipulation and practice. At the end of each week, place the cards together on a ring, and neatly store them in a shoe organizer that has clear pockets. Students can play games with the cards independently or with partners. It will make a big difference in their learning!

- Display only the words in the pocket chart. Read each word, and have students repeat it so their pronunciation is correct. Clap the number of syllables while rereading the words again. Read one definition at a time so students can apply logic and deduction to figure out which word it defines.

- After students have had the opportunity to pronounce the words correctly several times, invite them to write the words on the board with the correct syllable breaks.

Vocabulary Sort (Day 2)

Following the list of prefixes or suffixes and their definitions is a list of the same ten words and definitions mixed up and arranged on cut-apart slips of paper. This activity is intended to provide hands-on practice with the words.

- Copy a class set of Vocabulary Sort cards on construction paper or tagboard, cut apart the words and definitions, and place each set in a resealable plastic bag or small envelope. (You may want to laminate the cards for greater durability.) Have students independently match the words and definitions. Invite them to check their work by referring to their word list.

- Give each student a large envelope to store his or her Vocabulary Sort cards in after taking the quiz for that lesson. Have students add sets of cards to this collection all year long. At least once every two weeks, give students time to match up all of the prefixes, suffixes, and definitions they have learned. Although this will be challenging, the review will enhance students' vocabulary as they continue to use words they learned in previous lessons.

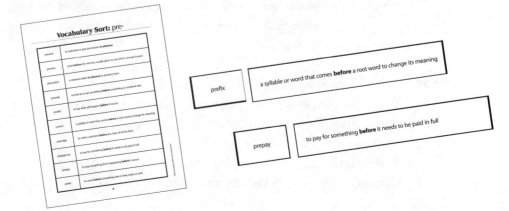

Read-Around Review (Days 3–4)

This set of cards includes definitions for all ten words that broaden the definition and apply more specifically to a practical context. Use these cards to play an interactive game with your students.

- Copy a set of cards on construction paper or tagboard for each small group of students. Cut apart the cards, and laminate them. Place each set of cards in an envelope, and write the title (e.g., *pre-*) on it. Give each group a set of cards so that each student has several cards. Read aloud each student's cards, and then have students silently read their cards at least five times. Discuss each question and corresponding answer so students are familiar and comfortable with all the cards. Tell the group that the student who has the clue card that says *I have the first card* will begin the game by reading aloud his or her card. After the first card is read aloud, have the student with the answer to the clue read aloud his or her card. Tell students to continue until they get back to the first card. (The game ends after a student reads *Who has the first card?* and a student answers *I have the first card.*) Have students use these cards for ongoing review, reading different cards each time they play.

Games (Days 1, 3, 4, 5)

- **Around the World:** Display the words in a pocket chart, and hold the definitions in your hand. Have students stand in 2–5 lines behind each other. Read a definition. The first student to say the matching word moves to the back of the line. Continue until each student has had several turns. This game is terrific for review weeks when you can use many different sets of prefixes or suffixes. (Store cards on rings for easy flipping.)
- **VOCABO:** Give each student a blank piece of paper. Have students draw lines to make a 4 x 4 grid of boxes (three lines across and three lines down). Tell them to write the vocabulary words and prefixes in any boxes they want as you say the words. Say one word at a time. Have students repeat it. Spell it out for them to write down by syllables. Include words studied in previous lessons for ongoing review. (Students love having a "free space" on their board!) After students' boards are filled in, play as you would play BINGO.
- **Vocabulary Race:** Put all of the words and definitions in a pocket chart. Invite two students to go up to the pocket chart. Give each student half of the definitions or words. Set a timer, and say *GO!* Have the students race to match up all of their words and definitions. Invite the remaining students to sit at their desks and watch for errors. Invite students to raise their hands to offer help.

Assessment (Day 5)

- **Vocabulary Quiz:** Use the 15-question quiz at the end of each lesson to assess students' learning. The quizzes include fill-in-the-bubble and fill-in-the-blank questions to help prepare students for standardized tests.
- **Review Test:** A 15-question review test follows every two lessons. Each test assesses students' knowledge using a fill-in-the-bubble format.

Read-Around Review: pre-

I have the first card.
Who has the word that describes what you do when you watch the movie
clips for upcoming movies **before** your real movie starts?

I have the word **preview.**
Who has the word that describes what happens when you pay
for something **before** you really need to?

I have the word **prepay.**
Who has the word that describes what your mother does when
she says you may spend the night at a friend's house next weekend?

I have the word **preapprove.**
Who has the word that describes how you say what will happen in a story **before** you read?

I have the word **predict.**
Who has the word that describes how you make a decision **before** you know all the information?

I have the word **prejudge.**
Who has the word that means a measure taken **in advance** to prevent harm?

I have the word **precaution.**
Who has the word that describes the part of a word that comes
before the root word and changes the meaning?

I have the word **prefix.**
Who has the word that describes what most teachers give **before** teaching a new
topic so that they know what they need to spend the most time teaching?

I have the word **pretest.**
Who has the word that describes trying to stop something **before** it happens?

I have the word **prevent.**
Who has the prefix that means **before** or **in advance**?

I have the prefix **pre-,** which means **before** or **in advance.**
Who has the word that describes when something comes **before** something else?

I have the word **precede.**
Who has the first card?

Prefixes and Suffixes © 2004 Creative Teaching Press

Name _____   Date _____

Vocabulary Quiz: pre-

Shade in the bubble for the correct word.

Ⓐ ● Ⓒ Ⓓ **1.** You do this when you make up your mind without knowing all the facts.
  A) predict   **B)** prejudge   **C)** premature   **D)** preview

Ⓐ Ⓑ ● Ⓓ **2.** This is something you see before anyone else or before the main attraction.
  A) precaution   **B)** prearrange   **C)** preview   **D)** premature

● Ⓑ Ⓒ Ⓓ **3.** This is a syllable that is at the beginning of a word that changes its meaning.
  A) prefix   **B)** precaution   **C)** precede   **D)** precaution

Ⓐ Ⓑ Ⓒ ● **4.** This is what good readers do before they begin reading.
  A) precede   **B)** prejudge   **C)** prearrange   **D)** predict

Ⓐ Ⓑ ● Ⓓ **5.** This is what your parents do when they agree to let you go to the movies with your friend in two weeks.
  A) prejudge   **B)** premature   **C)** preapprove   **D)** prefix

● Ⓑ Ⓒ Ⓓ **6.** Teachers often give this to figure out what their students already know.
  A) pretest   **B)** precede   **C)** prevent   **D)** precaution

Ⓐ Ⓑ ● Ⓓ **7.** You do this when you spend money for something before it is due.
  A) prearrange   **B)** precede   **C)** prepay   **D)** prevent

Ⓐ ● Ⓒ Ⓓ **8.** This is what we are studying.
  A) preschools   **B)** prefixes   **C)** precedes   **D)** previews

● Ⓑ Ⓒ Ⓓ **9.** You hear about these when people talk about how to avoid danger.
  A) precautions   **B)** previews   **C)** pretests   **D)** prepays

Ⓐ ● Ⓒ Ⓓ **10.** "An ounce of _____ is worth a pound of cure."
  A) prediction   **B)** prevention   **C)** prejudging   **D)** previews

Write the correct word on the line so the sentence makes sense.

11. What do you ___Predict___ will happen in the next chapter?

12. Javier ___Preceded___ his speech with a funny joke.

13. You can ___Prevent___ spreading germs by washing your hands often.

14. Four students got 100% on the spelling ___Pretests___, so they didn't have to take the final test on Friday.

15. You ___Pre Judge___ when you "judge a book by its cover."

Prefixes and Suffixes © 2004 Creative Teaching Press

Word List: post-

post-	after

Vocabulary	**Definitions**
postdate (v)	to write on something a date that comes **after** the real date
postgraduate (n)	a person who takes a college class **after** he or she has already graduated
posthumous (adj)	occurring or continuing **after** death; usually related to a book that is published **after** the author has died
postindustrial (n)	the time in society that came **after** the Industrial Revolution
postmark (n)	a mark printed across a stamp **after** it is received by the post office
postmeridian (adj)	taking place **after** noon; p.m.
postmortem (adj)	occurring or done **after** death; usually related to an examination of the body **after** it is dead
postpone (v)	to do something at a time or date **after** it was originally planned
postproduction (n)	the editing that is done **after** the movie, film, or video has been taped
postscript (n)	a comment, note, or thought written **after** the letter is finished; p.s.

Vocabulary Sort: post-

postscript	a mark printed across a stamp **after** it is received by the post office
postmeridian	occurring or continuing **after** death; usually related to a book that is published **after** the author has died
postgraduate	the editing that is done **after** the movie, film, or video has been taped
postdate	a comment, note, or thought written **after** the letter is finished; p.s.
postpone	the time in society that came **after** the Industrial Revolution
posthumous	to write on something a date that comes **after** the real date
postproduction	occurring or done **after** death; usually related to an examination of the body **after** it is dead
postmark	a person who takes a college class **after** he or she already graduated
postindustrial	to do something at a time or date **after** it was originally planned
postmortem	taking place **after** noon; p.m.

Read-Around Review: post-

I have the first card.
Who has the word that describes what you do when you have to change the
date of a picnic until **after** the planned date because it will be raining?

I have the word **postpone.**
Who has the word that describes the mark the postal clerk puts
across your stamp **after** your mail arrives at the post office?

I have the word **postmark.**
Who has the word that describes a type of examination that is sometimes
called an autopsy (that takes place **after** the person is dead)?

I have the word **postmortem.**
Who has the word that describes the period of time in
history that took place **after** the Industrial Revolution?

I have the word **postindustrial.**
Who has the word that describes something you might
add to a letter **after** you are done writing it?

I have the word **postscript.**
Who has the word that describes a book published **after** the author has passed away?

I have the word **posthumous.**
Who has the word that describes when the editors of movies
add clips and make changes **after** the movie was filmed?

I have the word **postproduction.**
Who has the word that describes when you write a date on something,
such as a check, for a date that is **after** the real date?

I have the word **postdate.**
Who has the word that describes the period of time in a day **after** 12:00 noon?

I have the word **postmeridian.**
Who has the word that would describe your teacher as a student returning to college?

I have the word **postgraduate.**
Who has the prefix that means **after?**

I have the prefix **post-.**
Who has the first card?

Name _____   Date _____

Vocabulary Quiz: post-

Shade in the bubble for the correct word.

Ⓐ Ⓑ Ⓒ Ⓓ   **1.** You do this when you write a date later than the actual day.
               A) postscript   **B)** postdate   **C)** postmark   **D)** postpone

Ⓐ Ⓑ Ⓒ Ⓓ   **2.** This is when you have to delay something because it has to take place at a later time.
               A) postpone   **B)** posthumous   **C)** postdate   **D)** postmark

Ⓐ Ⓑ Ⓒ Ⓓ   **3.** This is the time during which editing of movies takes place.
               A) posthumous   **B)** postproduction   **C)** postdate   **D)** postpone

Ⓐ Ⓑ Ⓒ Ⓓ   **4.** Which word describes the time period after the Industrial Revolution?
               A) postage   **B)** postindustrial   **C)** postdate   **D)** postpone

Ⓐ Ⓑ Ⓒ Ⓓ   **5.** After you finish college, you will become one of these.
               A) postscript   **B)** postproduction   **C)** postgraduate   **D)** postdater

Ⓐ Ⓑ Ⓒ Ⓓ   **6.** Sometimes after a death, family members might request this type of an exam.
               A) postmortem   **B)** posthumous   **C)** postmark   **D)** postponed

Ⓐ Ⓑ Ⓒ Ⓓ   **7.** The next time someone sends you a letter, look for one of these at the bottom.
               A) postmark   **B)** postgraduate   **C)** postdate   **D)** postscript

Ⓐ Ⓑ Ⓒ Ⓓ   **8.** The postmaster at the post office puts this mark on every piece of mail.
               A) postscript   **B)** postproduction   **C)** postmark   **D)** postdate

Ⓐ Ⓑ Ⓒ Ⓓ   **9.** Anytime after twelve o'clock noon would fit into this category.
               A) postmeridian   **B)** posthumous   **C)** postscript   **D)** postdated

Ⓐ Ⓑ Ⓒ Ⓓ   **10.** Which word describes the type of fame an author may achieve after his or her death?
               A) posthumous   **B)** postdated   **C)** postmarked   **D)** postponed

Write the correct word on the line so the sentence makes sense.

11. Do you really have to _____ the party? Maybe it won't be raining on Saturday.

12. The crew working on _____ added funny sound effects to the film.

13. Oh no! I forgot to add a _____ telling him my e-mail address!

14. I can prove that you sent me that bill late. The _____ shows that it was dated after the day the bill was due!

15. May I _____ the check for the date I will receive the furniture?

Review Test: pre- and post-

Shade in the bubble for the correct word.

Ⓐ Ⓑ Ⓒ Ⓓ **1.** I just bought a _____ phone card with $60.00 worth of calling time.
A) premature   **B)** postmarked   **C)** prepaid   **D)** postponed

Ⓐ Ⓑ Ⓒ Ⓓ **2.** When it is very hot, it is wise to _____ getting a headache by drinking lots of water.
A) prevent   **B)** preview   **C)** precaution   **D)** postmark

Ⓐ Ⓑ Ⓒ Ⓓ **3.** It is against the law to _____ someone before he or she gets a fair trial.
A) postmark   **B)** preview   **C)** prejudge   **D)** precede

Ⓐ Ⓑ Ⓒ Ⓓ **4.** We went to a sneak _____ of an upcoming film titled "Lost in the Galaxy."
A) preview   **B)** precede   **C)** preplan   **D)** postdate

Ⓐ Ⓑ Ⓒ Ⓓ **5.** What do you _____ will happen in the next chapter?
A) pretest   **B)** predict   **C)** postpone   **D)** postscript

Ⓐ Ⓑ Ⓒ Ⓓ **6.** We have learned the meanings of the _____ **pre-** and **post-.**
A) prefixes   **B)** postproductions   **C)** pretests   **D)** postdates

Ⓐ Ⓑ Ⓒ Ⓓ **7.** The _____ returned to college to study art history.
A) postgraduate   **B)** prejudge   **C)** postmark   **D)** postmeridian

Ⓐ Ⓑ Ⓒ Ⓓ **8.** The date is March 12, so the _____ on the envelope indicates the same date.
A) postdate   **B)** postmark   **C)** predate   **D)** prefix

Ⓐ Ⓑ Ⓒ Ⓓ **9.** The man needed to be _____ by the bank before he could buy the house.
A) postmortem   **B)** precautioned   **C)** preapproved   **D)** postponed

Ⓐ Ⓑ Ⓒ Ⓓ **10.** The music was added to the movie during _____.
A) postmeridian   **B)** postproduction   **C)** postponed   **D)** predated

Ⓐ Ⓑ Ⓒ Ⓓ **11.** The _____ included Sarah's new address so that I could write her back.
A) predate   **B)** precaution   **C)** postmark   **D)** postscript

Ⓐ Ⓑ Ⓒ Ⓓ **12.** Dance class ended at eight o'clock _____.
A) postmortem   **B)** postmeridian   **C)** pretimed   **D)** posthumous

Ⓐ Ⓑ Ⓒ Ⓓ **13.** You need to be aware of the safety _____ before taking medicine.
A) preventions   **B)** precautions   **C)** postdates   **D)** postmarks

Ⓐ Ⓑ Ⓒ Ⓓ **14.** Your _____ shows that you already know a lot about history!
A) postproduction   **B)** postmortem   **C)** preview   **D)** pretest

Ⓐ Ⓑ Ⓒ Ⓓ **15.** We will need to _____ skate night until next month.
A) preplan   **B)** postpone   **C)** preview   **D)** postdate

Word List: mono-

mono-   one

Vocabulary	Definitions
monochrome (adj)	having **one** color; a painting, design, photo, or outfit that is only **one** color or shades of **one** color
monocle (n)	an eyeglass for **one** eye
monolingual (adj)	speaking or writing only **one** language
monolith (n)	something made out of **one** single large block or piece of stone; **one** single stone monument
monologue (n)	a long speech given by **one** person
monophobia (n)	an abnormal fear of being the only **one** there; fear of being alone
monopoly (n)	control of a product or service by **one** company
monorail (n)	a track for subway or train cars that only has **one** rail
monosyllabic (adj)	having only **one** syllable
monotone (n)	a speech in which every word has **one** tone of voice

Prefixes and Suffixes © 2004 Creative Teaching Press

Vocabulary Sort: mono-

monotone	speaking or writing only **one** language
monochrome	a speech in which every word has **one** tone of voice
monolith	control of a product or service by **one** company
monophobia	having **one** color; a painting, design, photo, or outfit that is only **one** color or shades of **one** color
monorail	an eyeglass for **one** eye
monolingual	a long speech given by **one** person
monosyllabic	a track for subway or train cars that only has **one** rail
monopoly	having only **one** syllable
monocle	an abnormal fear of being the only **one** there; fear of being alone
monologue	something made out of **one** single large block or piece of stone; **one** single stone monument

Prefixes and Suffixes © 2004 Creative Teaching Press

Read-Around Review: mono-

I have the first card.
Who has the word that describes a product or service that is controlled by **one** company?

I have the word **monopoly.**
Who has the word that describes **one** large stone monument or single block of stone?

I have the word **monolith.**
Who has the prefix that means **one?**

I have the prefix **mono-,** which means **one.**
Who has the word that describes a long speech given by only **one** person?

I have the word **monologue.**
Who has the word that describes a fear of being the only **one** in a room or all alone?

I have the word **monophobia.**
Who has the word that describes a train that runs on only **one** track?

I have the word **monorail.**
Who has the word that describes a word with only **one** syllable?

I have the word **monosyllabic.**
Who has the word that describes a reader who needs
to work on reading with phrasing and fluency?

I have the word **monotone.**
Who has the word that describes an eyeglass that is held in front of **one** eye to see better?

I have the word **monocle.**
Who has the word that describes a person who only speaks **one** language?

I have the word **monolingual.**
Who has the word that describes a piece of art or a photograph
that is only **one** color or shades of that **one** color?

I have the word **monochrome.**
Who has the first card?

Name _____   Date _____

Vocabulary Quiz: mono-

Shade in the bubble for the correct word.

Ⓐ Ⓑ Ⓒ Ⓓ   **1.** What would you call a company that has almost all of the long distance phone service in one particular state?
　　　　　　　A) monorail　　　**B)** monopoly　　　**C)** monolith　　　**D)** monocle

Ⓐ Ⓑ Ⓒ Ⓓ   **2.** Some amusement parks and airports have this form of transportation.
　　　　　　　A) monolith　　　**B)** monotone　　　**C)** monocle　　　**D)** monorail

Ⓐ Ⓑ Ⓒ Ⓓ   **3.** The words *park, go,* and *yes* fit into this category.
　　　　　　　A) monosyllabic　　**B)** monologue　　**C)** monolingual　　**D)** monocle

Ⓐ Ⓑ Ⓒ Ⓓ   **4.** In our society today, it can be difficult to communicate if you are _____.
　　　　　　　A) monosyllabic　　**B)** monolingual　　**C)** monolith　　**D)** monochrome

Ⓐ Ⓑ Ⓒ Ⓓ   **5.** The talk show host always begins his show with a funny _____.
　　　　　　　A) monochrome　　**B)** monotone　　**C)** monologue　　**D)** monolith

Ⓐ Ⓑ Ⓒ Ⓓ   **6.** While on vacation, I saw the famous 8-foot-high _____.
　　　　　　　A) monologue　　**B)** monolith　　**C)** monotone　　**D)** monocle

Ⓐ Ⓑ Ⓒ Ⓓ   **7.** She loves to be in groups, since she suffers from _____.
　　　　　　　A) monophobia　　**B)** monochrome　　**C)** monologue　　**D)** monolith

Ⓐ Ⓑ Ⓒ Ⓓ   **8.** The gentlemen of the past used _____ to take a closer look at something.
　　　　　　　A) monoliths　　**B)** monologues　　**C)** monorails　　**D)** monocles

Ⓐ Ⓑ Ⓒ Ⓓ   **9.** The famous artist is known for his "blue period" in which many paintings were _____.
　　　　　　　A) monophobia　　**B)** monochrome　　**C)** monocles　　**D)** monotone

Ⓐ Ⓑ Ⓒ Ⓓ   **10.** Please use some expression in your voice so you don't sound _____.
　　　　　　　A) monotone　　**B)** monochrome　　**C)** monophobia　　**D)** monolith

Write the correct word on the line so the sentence makes sense.

11. The _____ student began taking Japanese as a second language.

12. A robot has a voice that usually sounds a bit _____.

13. The president's speech included a long _____.

14. Have you purchased your tickets for the _____ ride?

15. Which car company do you think has a _____ in the sports car industry?

Word List: poly-

poly-	many

Vocabulary	Definitions
polychromatic (adj)	having **many** different colors
polyclinic (n)	a hospital that treats **many** different kinds of diseases
polydactyl (adj)	having **many** fingers or toes (more than the normal number)
polyglot (n)	a person who knows how to speak, read, or write **many** languages
polygon (n)	a closed plane figure with **many** straight lines that connect
polygraph (n)	a machine that writes down **many** different changes in the body while the person answers questions; a lie detector test
polyhedron (n)	a solid figure with **many** sides, such as a pyramid
polymorphous (adj)	having or assuming **many** different forms
polysyllabic (adj)	having **many** syllables
polytheism (n)	the belief in **many** different gods

Prefixes and Suffixes © 2004 Creative Teaching Press

Vocabulary Sort: poly-

polygon	a closed plane figure with **many** straight lines that connect
polysyllabic	a solid figure with **many** sides, such as a pyramid
polychromatic	having **many** different colors
polydactyl	a person who knows how to speak, read, or write **many** languages
polygraph	having **many** syllables
polymorphous	a hospital that treats **many** different kinds of diseases
polytheism	having **many** fingers or toes (more than the normal number)
polyhedron	having or assuming **many** different forms
polyglot	the belief in **many** different gods
polyclinic	a machine that writes down **many** different changes in the body while the person answers questions; a lie detector test

Prefixes and Suffixes © 2004 Creative Teaching Press

Read-Around Review: poly-

I have the first card.
Who has the prefix that means **many** and is the opposite of **mono-?**

I have the prefix **poly-,** which means **many.**
Who has the word that means a **many**-sided solid figure, such as a pyramid?

I have the word **polyhedron.**
Who has the word that describes a painting that uses **many** colors?

I have the word **polychromatic.**
Who has the word that describes words that have **many** syllables?

I have the word **polysyllabic.**
Who has the word that is a machine that measures **many** basic body functions,
such as blood pressure and pulse, and writes down the results?

I have the word **polygraph.**
Who has the word that names a figure we learned about in math that has **many** sides?

I have the word **polygon.**
Who has the word that names the belief in **many** different gods?

I have the word **polytheism.**
Who has the word that describes a person who can speak or write in **many** different languages?

I have the word **polyglot.**
Who has the word that means to have or assume **many** different forms?

I have the word **polymorphous.**
Who has the word that describes the place where doctors and nurses
help people who come in with **many** different kinds of diseases?

I have the word **polyclinic.**
Who has the word that would be used to describe an animal
that was born with **many** toes—perhaps twelve?

I have the word **polydactyl.**
Who has the first card?

Prefixes and Suffixes © 2004 Creative Teaching Press

Name _____   Date _____

Vocabulary Quiz: poly-

Shade in the bubble for the correct word.

Ⓐ Ⓑ Ⓒ Ⓓ   **1.** Which word would be used to describe a monkey born with seven fingers?
A) polyglot   **B)** polydactyl   **C)** polyhedron   **D)** polygon

Ⓐ Ⓑ Ⓒ Ⓓ   **2.** How would you describe a bedspread designed with many different colors?
A) polyhedron   **B)** polygraphic   **C)** polychromatic   **D)** polygon

Ⓐ Ⓑ Ⓒ Ⓓ   **3.** If you went to Egypt, you would see many of these.
A) polyhedrons   **B)** polygraphs   **C)** polygons   **D)** polyglots

Ⓐ Ⓑ Ⓒ Ⓓ   **4.** Which word would best describe the word *unrealistic*?
A) polysyllabic   **B)** polydactyl   **C)** polytheism   **D)** polyglot

Ⓐ Ⓑ Ⓒ Ⓓ   **5.** In ancient times, what was the belief system of the people?
A) polygraphic   **B)** polyhedron   **C)** polychromatic   **D)** polytheism

Ⓐ Ⓑ Ⓒ Ⓓ   **6.** When something takes on many forms it is called this.
A) polygraph   **B)** polymorphous   **C)** polytheism   **D)** polygraphic

Ⓐ Ⓑ Ⓒ Ⓓ   **7.** Which word describes a rectangle?
A) polychromatic   **B)** polygraph   **C)** polydactyl   **D)** polygon

Ⓐ Ⓑ Ⓒ Ⓓ   **8.** If someone thought you were lying, what type of test could they ask you to take?
A) polygraph   **B)** polyclinic   **C)** polyhedron   **D)** polysyllabic

Ⓐ Ⓑ Ⓒ Ⓓ   **9.** How would you describe an author of a book that was written in many different languages?
A) polytheism   **B)** polyglot   **C)** polyhedron   **D)** polychromatic

Ⓐ Ⓑ Ⓒ Ⓓ   **10.** Name the place that could help a lady with the flu, a girl with chicken pox, and a man with cancer.
A) polyclinic   **B)** polyhedron   **C)** polyglot   **D)** polydactyl

Write the correct word on the line so the sentence makes sense.

11. What is the perimeter of that _____?

12. Good readers examine parts of _____ words to help them understand their meaning.

13. Some dinosaurs were _____, that is, they had many fingers.

14. That _____ painting sure brightens up the room!

15. My uncle is a _____, since he can read, write, and speak Chinese, Spanish, English, and Cantonese.

Review Test: mono- and poly-

Shade in the bubble for the correct word.

Ⓐ Ⓑ Ⓒ Ⓓ   **1.** Since it was so rare, the newspapers crowded to take pictures of the little girl who was born _____.

        A) polydactyl   **B)** polytheism   **C)** monotone   **D)** monosyllabic

Ⓐ Ⓑ Ⓒ Ⓓ   **2.** My family believes in only one god, but the ancient Greeks and Romans believed in _____.

        A) polytheism   **B)** polyglots   **C)** monophobia   **D)** monotheism

Ⓐ Ⓑ Ⓒ Ⓓ   **3.** Right now I am monolingual, but in the future I hope to become a _____.

        A) polyhedron   **B)** polyglot   **C)** monoglot   **D)** polygraph

Ⓐ Ⓑ Ⓒ Ⓓ   **4.** It is illegal in business today to have a _____ in an industry.

        A) polyclinic   **B)** monopoly   **C)** monolith   **D)** polygon

Ⓐ Ⓑ Ⓒ Ⓓ   **5.** Is that really a work of art? It's all black! It's simply too _____!

        A) polychromatic   **B)** polysyllabic   **C)** monosyllabic   **D)** monochrome

Ⓐ Ⓑ Ⓒ Ⓓ   **6.** The man had to take a _____ test before the trial. His pulse, breathing, and blood pressure showed that he was lying.

        A) polygraph   **B)** monograph   **C)** polyhedron   **D)** monologue

Ⓐ Ⓑ Ⓒ Ⓓ   **7.** If you know your prefixes, suffixes, and root meanings, then you can understand most _____ words.

        A) monosyllabic   **B)** monocle   **C)** polysyllabic   **D)** polyclinic

Ⓐ Ⓑ Ⓒ Ⓓ   **8.** When readers are _____ you can tell they are not enjoying the story.

        A) polytone   **B)** monotone   **C)** monodactyl   **D)** polyglot

Ⓐ Ⓑ Ⓒ Ⓓ   **9.** Since Trevor has been cured of _____, he can now stay home alone and not feel frightened.

        A) polytheism   **B)** monotone   **C)** monochromatic   **D)** monophobia

Ⓐ Ⓑ Ⓒ Ⓓ   **10.** The speaker's opening _____ was so exciting that everyone stood up and clapped for him.

        A) polyglot   **B)** monologue   **C)** polygons   **D)** monolith

Ⓐ Ⓑ Ⓒ Ⓓ   **11.** People today wear glasses on both of their eyes instead of a _____ on one eye when they need to read the morning paper.

        A) monocle   **B)** monolith   **C)** polyhedron   **D)** monologue

Ⓐ Ⓑ Ⓒ Ⓓ   **12.** The prefix **mono-** means _____.

        A) before   **B)** after   **C)** one   **D)** many

Ⓐ Ⓑ Ⓒ Ⓓ   **13.** The prefix **poly-** means _____.

        A) before   **B)** after   **C)** one   **D)** many

Ⓐ Ⓑ Ⓒ Ⓓ   **14.** The prefix **post-** means _____.

        A) before   **B)** after   **C)** one   **D)** many

Ⓐ Ⓑ Ⓒ Ⓓ   **15.** The prefix **pre-** means _____.

        A) before   **B)** after   **C)** one   **D)** many

Word List: uni-

uni-	one

Vocabulary	**Definitions**
unicellular (adj)	having only **one** cell
unicorn (n)	a horse-like fabled animal that has **one** horn growing out of the middle of its forehead
unicycle (n)	a **one**-wheeled vehicle on which the rider sits and pedals
unidirectional (adj)	moving in only **one** direction
unify (v)	to join together into **one** group
unilateral (adj)	**one** sided
unique (adj)	**one** of a kind; unusual or rare
unison (n)	an instance of saying the same words or sounds at the same time; a group that sounds like **one**
unit (n)	**one** group
unitard (n)	a **one**-piece leotard and tights combination

Prefixes and Suffixes © 2004 Creative Teaching Press

Vocabulary Sort: uni-

unicorn	**one** of a kind; unusual or rare
unicycle	a **one**-piece leotard and tights combination
unison	moving in only **one** direction
unilateral	**one** group
unique	a **one**-wheeled vehicle on which the rider sits and pedals
unify	having only **one** cell
unidirectional	**one** sided
unitard	an instance of saying the same words or sounds at the same time; a group that sounds like **one**
unit	a horse-like fabled animal that has **one** horn growing out of the middle of its forehead
unicellular	to join together into **one** group

Prefixes and Suffixes © 2004 Creative Teaching Press

Read-Around Review: uni-

I have the first card.
Who has the word that names the very tricky **one**-wheeled vehicle
that some people learn to ride without holding on to anything?

I have the word **unicycle.**
Who has the word that describes how the wind would
blow if it only blew to the north in a storm?

I have the word **unidirectional.**
Who has the word that describes a mythical creature that is said
to have **one** spiral horn coming out of the top of its head?

I have the word **unicorn.**
Who has the word that describes how a choir singing the
chorus of a song together would sound?

I have the word **unison.**
Who has the word that names a group of soldiers that work together like **one** team?

I have the word **unit.**
Who has the word that describes how a person might think
if he or she doesn't hear both sides of a story?

I have the word **unilateral.**
Who has the word that describes the act of joining together to reach a common goal?

I have the word **unify.**
Who has the word that describes a person who is the only **one** who has a particular quality?

I have the word **unique.**
Who has the word that describes a **one**-piece outfit a ballerina might wear?

I have the word **unitard.**
Who has the prefix that means **one?**

I have the prefix **uni-,** which means **one.**
Who has the word that describes something that has only **one** cell?

I have the word **unicellular.**
Who has the first card?

Prefixes and Suffixes © 2004 Creative Teaching Press

Name _____   Date _____

Vocabulary Quiz: uni-

Shade in the bubble for the correct word.

Ⓐ Ⓑ Ⓒ Ⓓ   **1.** Which word describes how there is only one "you"?
         A) unilateral   **B)** unison   **C)** unit   **D)** unique

Ⓐ Ⓑ Ⓒ Ⓓ   **2.** Which word could describe a discussion in which only one person talks and listens?
         A) unitard   **B)** unilateral   **C)** unison   **D)** unicellular

Ⓐ Ⓑ Ⓒ Ⓓ   **3.** The original thirteen colonies decided to do this in the late 1700s when they became the United States of America.
         A) unison   **B)** unit   **C)** unilateral   **D)** unify

Ⓐ Ⓑ Ⓒ Ⓓ   **4.** What word describes an organism with only one cell?
         A) unicellular   **B)** unilateral   **C)** united   **D)** unique

Ⓐ Ⓑ Ⓒ Ⓓ   **5.** This creature looks like a horned horse.
         A) unicorn   **B)** unitard   **C)** unicycle   **D)** unit

Ⓐ Ⓑ Ⓒ Ⓓ   **6.** A clown often rides on this at the circus.
         A) unicellular   **B)** unitard   **C)** unicorn   **D)** unicycle

Ⓐ Ⓑ Ⓒ Ⓓ   **7.** This word would best describe a one-way street.
         A) unicycle   **B)** unidirectional   **C)** unit   **D)** unique

Ⓐ Ⓑ Ⓒ Ⓓ   **8.** This one-piece outfit is often worn by dancers.
         A) unilateral   **B)** unitard   **C)** unique   **D)** unison

Ⓐ Ⓑ Ⓒ Ⓓ   **9.** A group often says the Pledge of Allegiance together or in _____.
         A) unique   **B)** unison   **C)** unicellular   **D)** unidirectional

Ⓐ Ⓑ Ⓒ Ⓓ   **10.** Which word can be used to describe almost anything that is put together into a group?
         A) unit   **B)** unison   **C)** unicorn   **D)** unique

Write the correct word on the line so the sentence makes sense.

11. Can you ride a _____, a bicycle, or a tricycle?

12. We will all sing the national anthem in _____ before the baseball game.

13. What a _____ idea! I've never heard it before!

14. Do you believe that _____ were ever alive? Do you think they were related to horses?

15. There is a _____ path to the cafeteria from our classroom.

Prefixes and Suffixes © 2004 Creative Teaching Press

Word List: bi-

bi-	two

Vocabulary	Definitions
bicolor (adj)	having **two** different colors
bicuspid (n)	a **two**-pointed tooth located in the side of the jaw
bicycle (n)	a vehicle with **two** wheels
biennial (adj)	happening every **two** years
bifocals (n)	eyeglasses with lenses that have **two** different sections—for seeing close up and far away
bilingual (adj)	able to speak **two** different languages
bimonthly (adj)	happening every **two** months
biped (n)	a **two**-footed creature
biplane (n)	an airplane with **two** pairs of wings
biweekly (adj)	happening every **two** weeks

Vocabulary Sort: bi-

biweekly	a **two**-footed creature
biped	a **two**-pointed tooth located in the side of the jaw
bilingual	eyeglasses with lenses that have **two** different sections—for seeing close up and far away
biennial	happening every **two** months
bicycle	having **two** different colors
biplane	happening every **two** years
bimonthly	happening every **two** weeks
bifocals	an airplane with **two** pairs of wings
bicuspid	able to speak **two** different languages
bicolor	a vehicle with **two** wheels

Prefixes and Suffixes © 2004 Creative Teaching Press

Read-Around Review: bi-

I have the first card.
Who has the word that describes a person who can speak both Spanish and English?

I have the word **bilingual.**
Who has the word that describes a tooth that has **two** points and is also known as a premolar?

I have the word **bicuspid.**
Who has the word that means a method of transportation with **two** wheels?

I have the word **bicycle.**
Who has the word that describes a piece of art that is painted with only red and blue paint?

I have the word **bicolor.**
Who has the word that means any living thing with **two** legs?

I have the word **biped.**
Who has the word that describes how a magazine might arrive at your home **twice** a month?

I have the word **biweekly.**
Who has the prefix that means **two?**

I have the prefix **bi-,** which means **two.**
Who has the word that means a plane with **two** pairs of wings?

I have the word **biplane.**
Who has the word that describes a magazine that you
would expect to get in the mail six times a year?

I have the word **bimonthly.**
Who has the word that means a pair of glasses with **two** parts to the lenses.

I have the word **bifocals.**
Who has the word that describes something that occurs every **two** years?

I have the word **biennial.**
Who has the first card?

Prefixes and Suffixes © 2004 Creative Teaching Press

Name _____   Date _____

Vocabulary Quiz: bi-

Shade in the bubble for the correct word.

Ⓐ Ⓑ Ⓒ Ⓓ   **1.** This word describes anything that consists of two colors.
   A) bichrome   **B)** bicolor   **C)** bilingual   **D)** biped

Ⓐ Ⓑ Ⓒ Ⓓ   **2.** What would you call a vehicle that has two wheels?
   A) biwheel   **B)** biped   **C)** bilingual   **D)** bicycle

Ⓐ Ⓑ Ⓒ Ⓓ   **3.** Dentists sometimes have to pull these out.
   A) bifocals   **B)** bipeds   **C)** bicuspids   **D)** bicycles

Ⓐ Ⓑ Ⓒ Ⓓ   **4.** A duck would be one of these.
   A) biplane   **B)** bicolor   **C)** biped   **D)** biweekly

Ⓐ Ⓑ Ⓒ Ⓓ   **5.** If you are this, then you have the ability to speak more than one language.
   A) bilingual   **B)** biennial   **C)** biped   **D)** bifocaled

Ⓐ Ⓑ Ⓒ Ⓓ   **6.** Some celebrations are described as being this since they occur every other year.
   A) biennial   **B)** bimonthly   **C)** biweekly   **D)** biped

Ⓐ Ⓑ Ⓒ Ⓓ   **7.** Does your grandma need these special glasses to be able to see all day?
   A) bilinguals   **B)** bicolors   **C)** bifocals   **D)** bicuspids

Ⓐ Ⓑ Ⓒ Ⓓ   **8.** Magazines that arrive in your mailbox every other month are this.
   A) biyearly   **B)** biweekly   **C)** bimonthly   **D)** bicolor

Ⓐ Ⓑ Ⓒ Ⓓ   **9.** Which word is a transportation vehicle with two pairs of wings?
   A) bicycle   **B)** biplane   **C)** bicuspid   **D)** biped

Ⓐ Ⓑ Ⓒ Ⓓ   **10.** Something that arrives in your mailbox 26 times a year is this.
   A) bimonthly   **B)** biennial   **C)** bilingual   **D)** biweekly

Write the correct word on the line so the sentence makes sense.

11. I need a pair of _____! I can't see far away or close up. I don't want to wear two different pairs of glasses!

12. Are you _____? Because if you can speak two languages, you will have more job opportunities than someone who is not.

13. The _____ book club sends my grandma a new book six times a year.

14. Our town's local "Hoppin' Days Celebration" is _____, since it's only celebrated on even-numbered years.

15. The animal kingdom is full of many _____.

Review Test: uni- and bi-

Shade in the bubble for the correct word.

Ⓐ Ⓑ Ⓒ Ⓓ   **1.** My eye doctor just made me a new pair of _____, so I can see both close up and far away.
     A) monocles   **B)** monofocals   **C)** bifocals   **D)** bicuspids

Ⓐ Ⓑ Ⓒ Ⓓ   **2.** The choir sang each song in perfect _____.
     A) bicolor   **B)** unison   **C)** biped   **D)** unify

Ⓐ Ⓑ Ⓒ Ⓓ   **3.** It is better to be _____ than to just speak one language.
     A) bilingual   **B)** unified   **C)** biennial   **D)** unique

Ⓐ Ⓑ Ⓒ Ⓓ   **4.** I am _____ and special.
     A) biped   **B)** unique   **C)** unit   **D)** biennial

Ⓐ Ⓑ Ⓒ Ⓓ   **5.** The Fruit of the Month Club delivers _____ shipments of fresh fruit (every other week).
     A) bimonthly   **B)** unilateral   **C)** unit   **D)** biweekly

Ⓐ Ⓑ Ⓒ Ⓓ   **6.** You have to pay close attention when driving _____ streets.
     A) unidirectional   **B)** bicuspid   **C)** bicycle   **D)** unicycle

Ⓐ Ⓑ Ⓒ Ⓓ   **7.** Every year, students _____ to help with disadvantaged children.
     A) biplane   **B)** unify   **C)** unitard   **D)** biped

Ⓐ Ⓑ Ⓒ Ⓓ   **8.** If you are a risk taker, you might try to fly in a _____ someday.
     A) unicycle   **B)** bicycle   **C)** unicorn   **D)** biplane

Ⓐ Ⓑ Ⓒ Ⓓ   **9.** The _____ contract was unfair to one of the companies.
     A) unilateral   **B)** biennial   **C)** unicellular   **D)** biped

Ⓐ Ⓑ Ⓒ Ⓓ   **10.** The large wheel on the _____ could hold a person who weighs up to 200 pounds.
     A) bicycle   **B)** unicorn   **C)** unicycle   **D)** biped

Ⓐ Ⓑ Ⓒ Ⓓ   **11.** What does the prefix **uni-** mean?
     A) one   **B)** two   **C)** before   **D)** after

Ⓐ Ⓑ Ⓒ Ⓓ   **12.** What does the prefix **bi-** mean?
     A) one   **B)** two   **C)** before   **D)** after

Ⓐ Ⓑ Ⓒ Ⓓ   **13.** What do you think **lateral** means in the word *unilateral*?
     A) monthly   **B)** sided   **C)** group   **D)** end

Ⓐ Ⓑ Ⓒ Ⓓ   **14.** What do you think **lingual** means in the word *bilingual*?
     A) two   **B)** smart   **C)** share   **D)** language

Ⓐ Ⓑ Ⓒ Ⓓ   **15.** What do you think **ped** means in the word *biped*?
     A) foot   **B)** two   **C)** walk   **D)** creature

Word List: tri-

tri-	three

Vocabulary	Definitions
triangle (n)	a **three**-sided figure
triathlon (n)	a race that combines **three** activities—swimming, bicycling, and running
triceratops (n)	a dinosaur with **three** horns—two long horns above the eyes and one short horn on the nose
tricycle (n)	a vehicle with **three** wheels
trilateral (adj)	having or involving **three** sides, countries, or parties
trilingual (adj)	able to speak **three** different languages
trilogy (n)	**three** related plays or novels
trio (n)	a group of **three** people or things
tripod (n)	a **three**-legged stool, table, or stand used to hold things, such as a camera
trisect (v)	to cut into **three** parts

Prefixes and Suffixes © 2004 Creative Teaching Press

Vocabulary Sort: tri-

trisect	able to speak **three** different languages
trilogy	to cut into **three** parts
triathlon	having or involving **three** sides, countries, or parties
tripod	a **three**-sided figure
tricycle	a **three**-legged stool, table, or stand used to hold things, such as a camera
trilateral	**three** related plays or novels
trio	a race that combines **three** activities—swimming, bicycling, and running
triangle	a dinosaur with **three** horns—two long horns above the eyes and one short horn on the nose
triceratops	a vehicle with **three** wheels
trilingual	a group of **three** people or things

Read-Around Review: tri-

I have the first card.
Who has the word that describes a person who can speak **three** languages?

I have the word **trilingual.**
Who has the word that describes an agreement between **three** people?

I have the word **trilateral.**
Who has the word that describes the **three**-legged item you
would use to hold a camera in place to take a picture?

I have the word **tripod.**
Who has the name of the athletic event that includes **three**
activities—biking, swimming, and running?

I have the word **triathlon.**
Who has the word that names a dinosaur with **three** horns?

I have the word **triceratops.**
Who has the word that names a group of **three** people who sing together?

I have the word **trio.**
Who has the prefix that means **three?**

I have the prefix **tri-,** which means **three.**
Who has the word that names the **three**-sided shape we study in math?

I have the word **triangle.**
Who has the word that names a **three**-wheeled vehicle children ride?

I have the word **tricycle.**
Who has the word that could describe what you do if you cut a candy bar into **three** equal parts?

I have the word **trisect.**
Who has the word that names a **three**-part series of books or plays?

I have the word **trilogy.**
Who has the first card?

Prefixes and Suffixes © 2004 Creative Teaching Press

Name _____   Date _____

Vocabulary Quiz: tri-

Shade in the bubble for the correct word.

Ⓐ Ⓑ Ⓒ Ⓓ   **1.** This three-horned reptile is now extinct.
       A) tricuspid   **B)** triceratops   **C)** trilogy   **D)** trisect

Ⓐ Ⓑ Ⓒ Ⓓ   **2.** What do you call a set of three plays or novels that go together?
       A) trilogy   **B)** tripod   **C)** tricycle   **D)** trio

Ⓐ Ⓑ Ⓒ Ⓓ   **3.** What is the name of the item that has three legs and can be attached to a camera for taking pictures.
       A) tripod   **B)** trilogy   **C)** tricycle   **D)** triangle

Ⓐ Ⓑ Ⓒ Ⓓ   **4.** What do we call someone who can speak German, French, and Spanish?
       A) bilingual   **B)** monolingual   **C)** trilingual   **D)** trisected

Ⓐ Ⓑ Ⓒ Ⓓ   **5.** What do you call something that is three-sided?
       A) trilateral   **B)** trilingual   **C)** tricycle   **D)** tripod

Ⓐ Ⓑ Ⓒ Ⓓ   **6.** The rectangular pizza was cut into three equal pieces. What did Amanda do to the pizza?
       A) trisect   **B)** tripod   **C)** trilogy   **D)** triathlon

Ⓐ Ⓑ Ⓒ Ⓓ   **7.** The man ran three miles every day and swam in his pool every morning. He was preparing for which big race?
       A) trilateral   **B)** triathlon   **C)** trisect   **D)** trilogy

Ⓐ Ⓑ Ⓒ Ⓓ   **8.** Name the vehicle with three wheels that young children ride.
       A) bicycle   **B)** unicycle   **C)** tricycle   **D)** tripod

Ⓐ Ⓑ Ⓒ Ⓓ   **9.** Name the three-sided figure that can be equilateral.
       A) triangle   **B)** trilogy   **C)** tricycle   **D)** trio

Ⓐ Ⓑ Ⓒ Ⓓ   **10.** If you and two friends get together to sing in a talent show, you can be called what?
       A) trilogy   **B)** trichromatic   **C)** triarchy   **D)** trio

Write the correct word on the line so the sentence makes sense.

11. Where is the _____ for my camera?

12. In science today, we are going to learn how to _____ a worm.

13. To be in a _____, you must be in excellent physical shape.

14. Luis' little brother is learning how to ride a _____ for the first time.

15. Have you read the _____ by Linda Guzman? The books are so exciting!

Word List: quad-

quad-	four

Vocabulary	**Definitions**
quadrangle (n)	a **four**-sided enclosure, usually surrounded by buildings
quadrant (n)	one out of **four** equal parts of a circle; one section of a **four**-section coordinate grid
quadrennial (adj)	happening every **four** years
quadriceps (n)	a muscle group consisting of **four** muscles that is located along the front of the thigh
quadrilateral (n)	a plane figure in geometry that has **four** sides (including square, rectangle, rhombus, parallelogram, and trapezoid)
quadrilingual (adj)	the ability to speak **four** languages
quadrisect (v)	to cut or divide into **four** equal parts
quadruped (n)	an animal with **four** feet
quadruple (v)	to create **four** times as much or as many of something
quadruplet (n)	a collection or group of **four;** one of **four** babies born from the same mother at the same time

Vocabulary Sort: quad-

quadruple	to cut or divide into **four** equal parts
quadrisect	the ability to speak **four** languages
quadrilateral	to create **four** times as much or as many of something
quadrennial	an animal with **four** feet
quadrangle	a plane figure in geometry that has **four** sides (including square, rectangle, rhombus, parallelogram, and trapezoid)
quadruplet	a muscle group consisting of **four** muscles that is located along the front of the thigh
quadruped	one out of **four** equal parts of a circle; one section of a **four**-section coordinate grid
quadrilingual	a collection or group of **four**; one of **four** babies born from the same mother at the same time
quadriceps	a **four**-sided enclosure, usually surrounded by buildings
quadrant	happening every **four** years

Prefixes and Suffixes © 2004 Creative Teaching Press

Read-Around Review: quad-

I have the first card.
Who has the prefix that means **four?**

I have the prefix **quad-,** which means **four.**
Who has the word that describes what you would be doing if you cut a square cake
in half one way and then in half the other way to create **four** equal pieces?

I have the word **quadrisect.**
Who has the word that describes a shape that has **four** sides?

I have the word **quadrilateral.**
Who has the word that describes a muscle group in your body that includes **four** muscles?

I have the word **quadriceps.**
Who has the word that describes an area that is surrounded by buildings on all **four** sides?

I have the word **quadrangle.**
Who has the word that describes a celebration that is enjoyed every **four** years?

I have the word **quadrennial.**
Who has the word that describes an animal (usually a mammal) that has **four** legs?

I have the word **quadruped.**
Who has the word that means you make **four** times as many of something?

I have the word **quadruple.**
Who has the word that describes a boy who is one of **four**
children born at the same time from the same mother?

I have the word **quadruplet.**
Who has the word that describes what a person could be called
if she can speak English, Spanish, Chinese, and Vietnamese?

I have the word **quadrilingual.**
Who has the word that describes one out of **four** equal sections of a circle
or a square, especially on a coordinate grid on which you plot points?

I have the word **quadrant.**
Who has the first card?

Prefixes and Suffixes © 2004 Creative Teaching Press

Name _____   Date _____

Vocabulary Quiz: quad-

Shade in the bubble for the correct word.

Ⓐ Ⓑ Ⓒ Ⓓ   **1.** This is how you could cut a gummy worm into four equal parts to share with your friends.
A) quadruped   **B)** quadrisect   **C)** quadruple   **D)** quadrant

Ⓐ Ⓑ Ⓒ Ⓓ   **2.** Your thigh muscles are called _____, since they are a group of four muscles.
A) quadriceps   **B)** quadrangle   **C)** quadruped   **D)** quadrennial

Ⓐ Ⓑ Ⓒ Ⓓ   **3.** This is one section of a four-section coordinate grid. It contains the positive *x* and positive *y* coordinates.
A) quadrilingual   **B)** quadruped   **C)** quadrangle   **D)** quadrant

Ⓐ Ⓑ Ⓒ Ⓓ   **4.** What do you call a four-sided shape?
A) quadrangle   **B)** quadrilateral   **C)** quadrilingual   **D)** quadruped

Ⓐ Ⓑ Ⓒ Ⓓ   **5.** Find the name of the area that has four sides with buildings around it.
A) quadrilateral   **B)** quadrilingual   **C)** quadruplet   **D)** quadrangle

Ⓐ Ⓑ Ⓒ Ⓓ   **6.** The Super Sock Festival is celebrated every four years in Socktown. How would you describe how often this festival is celebrated?
A) quadruplet   **B)** quadrilingual   **C)** quadrennial   **D)** quadruple

Ⓐ Ⓑ Ⓒ Ⓓ   **7.** If you get $5.00 in allowance each week and you have saved $20.00, this is what you were able to do to your savings.
A) quadruple   **B)** quadruped   **C)** quadrant   **D)** quadruplet

Ⓐ Ⓑ Ⓒ Ⓓ   **8.** Wow! I didn't know that Trenton could speak four languages! What is Trenton?
A) quadrilateral   **B)** quadrangle   **C)** quadrilingual   **D)** quadruplet

Ⓐ Ⓑ Ⓒ Ⓓ   **9.** Dogs, lions, rabbits, and elephants have something in common. They are all _____.
A) quadruplets   **B)** quadrilingual   **C)** quadrupeds   **D)** quadrants

Ⓐ Ⓑ Ⓒ Ⓓ   **10.** Linda has three sisters who look identical to her. They are all fifteen years old. What are they?
A) quadrupeds   **B)** quadruplets   **C)** quadrangles   **D)** quadrants

Write the correct word on the line so the sentence makes sense.

11. Most people only speak one or two languages. It is an unusual talent to be _____.

12. The _____ Hoptown Hoedown was celebrated in 1990, 1994, 1998, and 2002.

13. Mr. Math asked, "What is the perimeter of this _____?"

14. The Shishi Company is hoping to _____ the amount of money they make by next year by lowering prices to increase sales.

15. My mom decided to _____ the pizza so we could each have one of the equal-sized pieces.

Review Test: tri- and quad-

Shade in the bubble for the correct word.

Ⓐ Ⓑ Ⓒ Ⓓ   **1.** Did you hear about the paleontologist who found an ancient triceratops? How many horns were on the dinosaur?
    A) five   **B)** four   **C)** three   **D)** two

Ⓐ Ⓑ Ⓒ Ⓓ   **2.** Richard is quadrilingual. What can Richard do?
    A) ride a four-wheeled bike   **B)** speak four languages
    C) speak two languages   **D)** cut something into four pieces

Ⓐ Ⓑ Ⓒ Ⓓ   **3.** Shanelle tried to trisect her doughnut. She found it much harder than if she had quadrisected the doughnut. Which was harder?
    A) cutting it into two sections   **B)** cutting it into three sections
    C) cutting it into four sections   **D)** cutting it into five sections

Ⓐ Ⓑ Ⓒ Ⓓ   **4.** Panda is not really a panda. She's a black and white rabbit. She is also a _____.
    A) quadrant   **B)** triped   **C)** quadruped   **D)** trilogy

Ⓐ Ⓑ Ⓒ Ⓓ   **5.** The three singing sisters called themselves the Thompson _____.
    A) quartet   **B)** tripods   **C)** trio   **D)** quadruplets

Ⓐ Ⓑ Ⓒ Ⓓ   **6.** Mrs. Ling just had four new babies named Shiloh, Shelby, Lance, and Larry. They were all born on the same day. What were they?
    A) quadrupeds   **B)** quadruplets   **C)** triplets   **D)** tripods

Ⓐ Ⓑ Ⓒ Ⓓ   **7.** How many more sides does a quadrangle have than a triangle?
    A) four   **B)** three   **C)** two   **D)** one

Ⓐ Ⓑ Ⓒ Ⓓ   **8.** The perimeter of that trilateral shape is 12 inches. How long is each side?
    A) 2 inches   **B)** 4 inches   **C)** 3 inches   **D)** 6 inches

Ⓐ Ⓑ Ⓒ Ⓓ   **9.** By running every morning for three months, she was able to quadruple the number of laps she could run around the park in 15 minutes. What did she do?
    A) ran around the park four times   **B)** ran around the park three times
    C) ran four times as many laps   **D)** ran three times as many laps

Ⓐ Ⓑ Ⓒ Ⓓ   **10.** How many activities did the people in the triathlon have to do?
    A) two   **B)** three   **C)** four   **D)** five

Ⓐ Ⓑ Ⓒ Ⓓ   **11.** What does the prefix **quad-** mean?
    A) one   **B)** two   **C)** three   **D)** four

Ⓐ Ⓑ Ⓒ Ⓓ   **12.** The Triplet Trilogy included how many books?
    A) one   **B)** two   **C)** three   **D)** four

Ⓐ Ⓑ Ⓒ Ⓓ   **13.** What does the part **ennial** mean in the words *quadrennial* and *biennial*?
    A) 100   **B)** monthly   **C)** 10   **D)** yearly

Ⓐ Ⓑ Ⓒ Ⓓ   **14.** What do you think the part **lateral** means in the words *bilateral* and *trilateral*?
    A) books   **B)** sides   **C)** languages   **D)** years

Ⓐ Ⓑ Ⓒ Ⓓ   **15.** What do you think the part **sect** means in the words *bisect, trisect,* and *quadrisect*?
    A) equal   **B)** shape   **C)** cut   **D)** angles

Word List: co-, com-

co-, com-	together, with

Vocabulary	Definitions
coexist (v)	to live **together** without any problems; to be **together** in the same time or space
cohesive (adj)	sticking **together**
coincidence (n)	a sequence of events happening **together** that although accidental seems to have been planned or arranged
combine (v)	to put two things **together**
commiserate (v)	to feel sorry for someone, something, or a situation; to feel pity; to get **together with** someone to feel sadness
committee (n)	a group of people who meet **together** to discuss a topic
communication (n)	the act of talking **with** someone and discussing something **together**
community (n)	a place where people live **together**
compare (v)	to put things **together** to see how they are the same
compatible (adj)	able to live **together** and get along; things that can go **together** without problems

Prefixes and Suffixes © 2004 Creative Teaching Press

Vocabulary Sort: co-, com-

compatible	a sequence of events happening **together** that although accidental seems to have been planned or arranged
community	a group of people who meet **together** to discuss a topic
coexist	to put things **together** to see how they are the same
coincidence	a place where people live **together**
committee	to feel sorry for someone, something, or a situation; to feel pity; to get **together with** someone to feel sadness
combine	sticking **together**
cohesive	able to live **together** and get along; things that can go **together** without problems
compare	to put two things **together**
communication	the act of talking **with** someone and discussing something **together**
commiserate	to live **together** without any problems; to be **together** in the same time or space

44

Prefixes and Suffixes © 2004 Creative Teaching Press

Read-Around Review: co-, com-

I have the first card.
Who has the word that describes the unlikely event of two
unplanned things happening at the **same** time?

I have the word **coincidence.**
Who has the word that describes what you would be doing if you met
with a friend for lunch to discuss a sad event in both of your lives?

I have the word **commiserate.**
Who has the word that describes what you would be doing
if you mixed eggs and flour **together** to make cookies?

I have the word **combine.**
Who has the word that describes a group of people meeting **together**
to discuss a way to raise more money for our school?

I have the word **committee.**
Who has the word that describes two people who get along well **together,**
have the **same** interests, and love doing the same activities?

I have the word **compatible.**
Who has the word that describes how we talk **with** one another?

I have the word **communication.**
Who has the word that describes a water polo team that works **together** to achieve victories?

I have the word **cohesive.**
Who has the word that means a group of people living **together** in
the same area and sharing the resources that are available there?

I have the word **community.**
Who has the word that names how a friendly dog and a friendly rabbit
could live **together** in the same house without any problems?

I have the word **coexist.**
Who has the word that describes what you do when you try to find
three characteristics that you and your friend share **together?**

I have the word **compare.**
Who has the prefixes that mean **together** or **with?**

I have the prefixes **co-** and **com-,** which mean **together** or **with.**
Who has the first card?

Vocabulary Quiz: co-, com-

Shade in the bubble for the correct word.

Ⓐ Ⓑ Ⓒ Ⓓ   **1.** What word describes what our class is that enables us to get along so well?
        A) combine   **B)** commiserate   **C)** cohesive   **D)** committee

Ⓐ Ⓑ Ⓒ Ⓓ   **2.** If I ask you to research how our school is like another, what will you do?
        A) combine   **B)** compatible   **C)** commiserate   **D)** compare

Ⓐ Ⓑ Ⓒ Ⓓ   **3.** Discussing and listening are the basics of what skill?
        A) communication **B)** community   **C)** commiserate   **D)** committee

Ⓐ Ⓑ Ⓒ Ⓓ   **4.** Where do you live?
        A) committee   **B)** community   **C)** coincidence   **D)** commiserate

Ⓐ Ⓑ Ⓒ Ⓓ   **5.** If you are able to be at peace with others in spite of your differences, you can
        _____.
        A) coincidence   **B)** coexist   **C)** compatible   **D)** cohesive

Ⓐ Ⓑ Ⓒ Ⓓ   **6.** Erin was surprised when she saw Max and Fred at the restaurant. She didn't know they ate there. What was the event?
        A) commiserate   **B)** coincidence   **C)** cohesive   **D)** compatible

Ⓐ Ⓑ Ⓒ Ⓓ   **7.** The group was planning to clean up the beaches. They called themselves the Clean-Up _____.
        A) combination   **B)** commiserate   **C)** cohesive   **D)** committee

Ⓐ Ⓑ Ⓒ Ⓓ   **8.** The scientist mixed baking soda with vinegar. What did he do?
        A) commiserated   **B)** combined   **C)** coexisted   **D)** committee

Ⓐ Ⓑ Ⓒ Ⓓ   **9.** Often at a funeral you will see people do this.
        A) committee   **B)** communicate   **C)** commiserate   **D)** coexist

Ⓐ Ⓑ Ⓒ Ⓓ   **10.** Her grandparents have been married for 32 years. They get along great. What are they?
        A) coexisting   **B)** commiserating   **C)** comparing   **D)** compatible

Write the correct word on the line so the sentence makes sense.

11. The _____ included 70 people who want to stop the city from cutting down the trees.

12. The students at camp had to _____ in their cabins, even if they weren't friends.

13. The sisters began to _____ over the death of their pet fish.

14. Mrs. Solar told the class to _____ her garden to Mrs. Jackson's garden.

15. The park in the _____ was very crowded.

Word List: contra-, counter-

contra-, counter-   against, opposite

Vocabulary	Definitions
contraband (n)	anything that is **against** the law to buy or sell
contradict (v)	to express the **opposite**
contrarian (n)	a person who thinks differently from other people; a person who does the **opposite** of what is expected
contrary (adj)	completely different; **opposite** in nature, opinion, or action
contrast (v)	to look at different things to see how they are **opposites** or not related
counterbalance (n)	a weight used to balance an **opposite** weight
counterclockwise (adv)	in the direction that is **opposite** of the direction the hands on the clock move
counterexample (n)	an example used to support a claim or statement that is the **opposite** of another claim or statement
counterfeit (adj)	being the **opposite** of real; fake or artificial
counterintuitive (adj)	goes **against** your gut feeling or common sense

Prefixes and Suffixes © 2004 Creative Teaching Press

Vocabulary Sort: contra-, counter-

contrast	a person who thinks differently from other people; a person who does the **opposite** of what is expected
contrary	to look at different things to see how they are **opposites** or not related
contradict	an example used to support a claim or statement that is the **opposite** of another claim or statement
counterexample	being the **opposite** of real; fake or artificial
counterintuitive	a weight used to balance an **opposite** weight
contrarian	to express the **opposite**
counterfeit	goes **against** your gut feeling or common sense
contraband	in the direction that is **opposite** of the direction the hands on the clock move
counterclockwise	anything that is **against** the law to buy or sell
counterbalance	completely different; **opposite** in nature, opinion, or action

Prefixes and Suffixes © 2004 Creative Teaching Press

Read-Around Review: contra-, counter-

I have the first card.
Who has the prefixes that mean **against** or the **opposite?**

I have the prefixes **contra-** and **counter-.**
Who has the word that describes which direction you would be spinning
a top if it was the **opposite** of the way the hands on a clock move?

I have the word **counterclockwise.**
Who has the word that means a weight used to balance an **opposite** weight?

I have the word **counterbalance.**
Who has the word that describes what illegal or fake money is?

I have the word **counterfeit.**
Who has the word that is the **opposite** of when you compare how things are similar?

I have the word **contrast.**
Who has the word that names a person who always does the **opposite** of everyone else?

I have the word **contrarian.**
Who has the word that describes your behavior if you express the **opposite** of what you'll do.

I have the word **contradict.**
Who has the word that names illegal items that are brought into the United States?

I have the word **contraband.**
Who has the word that describes your opinion if it is different from everyone else's?

I have the word **contrary.**
Who has the word that names what you would have to give if you were in a
debate and someone just made a statement you didn't believe was correct?

I have the word **counterexample.**
Who has the word that means you do something that goes **against** your gut feeling?

I have the word **counterintuitive.**
Who has the first card?

Name _____   Date _____

Vocabulary Quiz: contra-, counter-

Shade in the bubble for the correct word.

Ⓐ Ⓑ Ⓒ Ⓓ   **1.** A person would be arrested if he were caught with this.
   A) contrast   **B)** counterintuitive   **C)** contrary   **D)** contraband

Ⓐ Ⓑ Ⓒ Ⓓ   **2.** Pressure from your friends can often cause you to do something that is _____.
   A) counterintuitive   **B)** contraption   **C)** contrarian   **D)** counterfeit

Ⓐ Ⓑ Ⓒ Ⓓ   **3.** "I disagree. I think air pollution is helpful not harmful." Which word would describe the person who said this?
   A) counterfeit   **B)** counterexample   **C)** contrary   **D)** contrast

Ⓐ Ⓑ Ⓒ Ⓓ   **4.** The weight was used to balance another weight.
   A) counterexample   **B)** contradictory   **C)** contrasting   **D)** counterbalance

Ⓐ Ⓑ Ⓒ Ⓓ   **5.** It is rude to _____ what someone is saying if you don't know all of the facts.
   A) contrary   **B)** counterfeit   **C)** contradict   **D)** contrast

Ⓐ Ⓑ Ⓒ Ⓓ   **6.** Which word describes the girl who wore pajamas to school just because she felt like it?
   A) contrarian   **B)** counterintuitive   **C)** counterfeit   **D)** contrast

Ⓐ Ⓑ Ⓒ Ⓓ   **7.** What are you trying to do when you identify ways that black bears are different from grizzly bears?
   A) counterexample   **B)** contrarian   **C)** contrast   **D)** counterfeit

Ⓐ Ⓑ Ⓒ Ⓓ   **8.** This type of money is made in the United States more often than in any other country.
   A) counterfeit   **B)** counterintuitive   **C)** contrarian   **D)** contraband

Ⓐ Ⓑ Ⓒ Ⓓ   **9.** The water in sinks and toilets in the countries south of the equator drains in this direction.
   A) counterclockwise   **B)** contrary   **C)** contrast   **D)** contraband

Ⓐ Ⓑ Ⓒ Ⓓ   **10.** The mayor said, "We have heard Mr. Olson's opinion on tax changes. What do you have to say to support your opinion, Mr. Guzman?" Mr. Guzman is running against Mr. Olson in the election. What will he provide?
   A) counterexample   **B)** contrarian   **C)** counterfeit   **D)** contrast

Write the correct word on the line so the sentence makes sense.

11. You are so _____! You never agree with the rest of us!

12. The United States created new $20.00 bills to help reduce the _____ money illegally created.

13. Do your parents ever _____ each other?

14. Some good advice in life is to never do anything that seems _____ to you.

15. In the times of the original thirteen colonies, Great Britain considered many food items to be _____.

Name _____   Date _____

Review Test: co-, com- and contra-, counter-

Shade in the bubble for the correct word.

Ⓐ Ⓑ Ⓒ Ⓓ   **1.** Jaiye and Mosha started to commiserate together when their favorite team lost the basketball semifinals. What did they do?
A) planned a party   **B)** canceled their plans
C) shared their sadness   **D)** laughed

Ⓐ Ⓑ Ⓒ Ⓓ   **2.** Lauren and Monica were best friends. When they wore the same outfit to school, everyone thought it was just a _____.
A) counterintuitive   **B)** coincidence   **C)** counterexample   **D)** committee

Ⓐ Ⓑ Ⓒ Ⓓ   **3.** Chan thought he bought a Monet painting. He was very upset when he discovered that it was _____.
A) contrarian   **B)** compatible
C) counterfeit   **D)** only a contraption

Ⓐ Ⓑ Ⓒ Ⓓ   **4.** Brenton told his mom, "You may think I'm tired, but it's quite the _____. I'm wide awake! It's only 11:30 at night!"
A) comparison   **B)** contradict   **C)** compatible   **D)** contrary

Ⓐ Ⓑ Ⓒ Ⓓ   **5.** When you bake a cake, you need to _____ all of the ingredients.
A) coexist   **B)** contrast   **C)** compare   **D)** combine

Ⓐ Ⓑ Ⓒ Ⓓ   **6.** He designed a machine to _____ the weights.
A) counterbalance   **B)** cohesive   **C)** committee   **D)** contrarian

Ⓐ Ⓑ Ⓒ Ⓓ   **7.** "Mr. Nguyen, I don't mean to _____ you, but I think the Declaration of Independence was signed in 1776 not 1774."
A) counterexample   **B)** contrast   **C)** contradict   **D)** compatible

Ⓐ Ⓑ Ⓒ Ⓓ   **8.** The whales and dolphins _____ in the ocean.
A) counterintuitive   **B)** coexist   **C)** contradict   **D)** compare

Ⓐ Ⓑ Ⓒ Ⓓ   **9.** Any army or navy unit must be _____.
A) a committee   **B)** a coincidence   **C)** cohesive   **D)** contrarian

Ⓐ Ⓑ Ⓒ Ⓓ   **10.** "Should we form a _____ to plan what to do on Principal Appreciation Day?" asked Mr. Arias.
A) communication   **B)** contrast   **C)** committee   **D)** contraption

Ⓐ Ⓑ Ⓒ Ⓓ   **11.** What do the prefixes **co-** and **com-** mean?
A) opposite   **B)** together   **C)** apart   **D)** meeting

Ⓐ Ⓑ Ⓒ Ⓓ   **12.** If your class sat in a circle and passed around a plate of cookies (which you love!), which way would you want the plate passed if it started with the girl on your left?
A) counterclockwise   **B)** clockwise   **C)** straight across   **D)** diagonally

Ⓐ Ⓑ Ⓒ Ⓓ   **13.** What do the prefixes **contra-** and **counter-** mean?
A) before   **B)** one   **C)** opposite   **D)** same

Ⓐ Ⓑ Ⓒ Ⓓ   **14.** Finish the analogy: compare : contrast :: _____ : different
A) unique   **B)** same   **C)** outside   **D)** Venn diagram

Ⓐ Ⓑ Ⓒ Ⓓ   **15.** The place that you live is called a _____.
A) committee   **B)** contraption   **C)** community   **D)** contraband

Word List: sub-

sub-	under, below

Vocabulary	Definitions
subconscious (adj)	not fully aware; occurring **below** your level of thinking and awareness
subcutaneous (adj)	**under** the skin
subdue (v)	to bring **under** control
subfreezing (adj)	**below** the freezing point
subirrigate (v)	to water something from **under** the ground
subject (v)	to put **under** someone else's control
submarine (n)	a watercraft that stays **under** water
submerge (v)	to put **under** water
subordinate (n)	a person who is **under** someone else in rank or importance
subway (n)	a passageway **under** the ground; an electric **under**ground railway

Prefixes and Suffixes © 2004 Creative Teaching Press

Vocabulary Sort: sub-

submerge	a person who is **under** someone else in rank or importance
subcutaneous	to put **under** someone else's control
subject	to water something from **under** the ground
subconscious	**under** the skin
subirrigate	to put **under** water
subway	to bring **under** control
subordinate	a watercraft that stays **under** water
subfreezing	not fully aware; occurring **below** your level of thinking and awareness
subdue	**below** the freezing point
submarine	a passageway **under** the ground; an electric **under**ground railway

Prefixes and Suffixes © 2004 Creative Teaching Press

Read-Around Review: sub-

I have the first card.
Who has the prefix that means **under?**

I have the prefix **sub-.**
Who has the word that describes a temperature that is **below** 32 degrees Fahrenheit?

I have the word **subfreezing.**
Who has the word that names the method of watering plants from
under the ground instead of using a sprinkler system?

I have the word **subirrigate.**
Who has the word that means that you put a person **under**
the rules and control of someone else?

I have the word **subject.**
Who has the word that names the vehicle of **under**water transportation
that is not seen from the top of the ocean?

I have the word **submarine.**
Who has the word that describes your level of awareness when
you do something without having to think about it?

I have the word **subconscious.**
Who has the word that could be used to describe an injury caused by a splinter?

I have the word **subcutaneous.**
Who has the word that means a type of transportation that runs **under** your city streets?

I have the word **subway.**
Who has the word that describes what a teacher is in comparison to a principal at school?

I have the word **subordinate.**
Who has the word that describes how you try to manage your feelings when you're upset?

I have the word **subdue.**
Who has the word that means to put something **under** the water?

I have the word **submerge.**
Who has the first card?

Prefixes and Suffixes © 2004 Creative Teaching Press

Vocabulary Quiz: sub-

Shade in the bubble for the correct word.

Ⓐ Ⓑ Ⓒ Ⓓ   **1.** Which word describes arctic temperatures throughout the year?
     A) submerge   **B)** subfreezing   **C)** subdue   **D)** subordinate

Ⓐ Ⓑ Ⓒ Ⓓ   **2.** Smiling when you are happy is this type of activity.
     A) subordinate   **B)** subcutaneous   **C)** subjected   **D)** subconscious

Ⓐ Ⓑ Ⓒ Ⓓ   **3.** Kendra tried to do this to her brother Garrett's rubber boat in the bathtub.
     A) subirrigate   **B)** subfreezing   **C)** submerge   **D)** subject

Ⓐ Ⓑ Ⓒ Ⓓ   **4.** The colonists were _____ to the rule of the British.
     A) subdued   **B)** subirrigated   **C)** subjected   **D)** subcutaneous

Ⓐ Ⓑ Ⓒ Ⓓ   **5.** Which word is the name of a water vessel that spends most of its time deep beneath the surface of the sea?
     A) submarine   **B)** submerge   **C)** subway   **D)** subconscious

Ⓐ Ⓑ Ⓒ Ⓓ   **6.** She tried to subdue her excitement so she wouldn't give the surprise away. What did she try to do?
     A) show her excitement   **B)** hide her excitement
     C) become more excited   **D)** make other people excited

Ⓐ Ⓑ Ⓒ Ⓓ   **7.** The carrot farmer decided to try a new _____ system.
     A) subordinate   **B)** subirrigation   **C)** subdued   **D)** subfreezing

Ⓐ Ⓑ Ⓒ Ⓓ   **8.** The school nurse could not remove the splinter since it was _____.
     A) subcutaneous   **B)** subordinate   **C)** subdued   **D)** subject

Ⓐ Ⓑ Ⓒ Ⓓ   **9.** The sergeant told his _____ what they needed to do.
     A) submerges   **B)** subordinates   **C)** submarines   **D)** subways

Ⓐ Ⓑ Ⓒ Ⓓ   **10.** What is the train under the ground called?
     A) subway   **B)** subfreezing   **C)** subordinate   **D)** subconscious

Write the correct word on the line so the sentence makes sense.

11. You are my _____. I don't have to do what YOU say!

12. The human body cannot survive in _____ temperatures for long.

13. The sinking ship began to _____.

14. When they were in New York City, they walked down a staircase that took them underground to ride the _____.

15. The cut was _____, but luckily it didn't require stitches.

Word List: super-, sur-

super-, sur-	over, above, beyond

Vocabulary	Definitions
superb (adj)	splendid; excellent; **beyond** the expected
superimpose (v)	to lay or place something **over** something else
superintendent (n)	a person with the highest power, power **above** everyone else's
superior (adj)	**above** average in quality; excellent
supervisor (n)	a person who stands **over** or **above** someone in rank; a manager in charge of someone else
surcharge (n)	an amount of money (charge) **over** and **above** what is already being paid
surplus (n)	a quantity or amount **over** and **above** what is actually needed; extra
surprise (n)	something that is **beyond** what is expected
surreal (adj)	**beyond** what is real or believable; bizarre
surtax (n)	an extra tax **beyond** the normal tax

Prefixes and Suffixes © 2004 Creative Teaching Press

Vocabulary Sort: super-, sur-

superintendent	an extra tax **beyond** the normal tax
superimpose	splendid; excellent; **beyond** the expected
supervisor	**beyond** what is real or believable; bizarre
surreal	**above** average in quality; excellent
surplus	a person who stands **over** or **above** someone in rank; a manager in charge of someone else
surprise	something that is **beyond** what is expected
superb	to lay or place something **over** something else
surtax	an amount of money (charge) **over** and **above** what is already being paid
surcharge	a quantity or amount **over** and **above** what is actually needed; extra
superior	a person with the highest power, power **above** everyone else's

Prefixes and Suffixes © 2004 Creative Teaching Press

Read-Around Review: super-, sur-

I have the first card.
Who has the word that is usually used to describe a painting or
art that is not realistic at all and even seems a little strange?

I have the word **surreal.**
Who has the word that describes how you make images
look like they are laying on top of each other in art?

I have the word **superimpose.**
Who has the word that describes the person with the most power in the school district?

I have the word **superintendent.**
Who has the word that names a tax **over** and **above** the tax you already pay?

I have the word **surtax.**
Who has the word that is usually used to describe a
party that is **beyond** what the person expects?

I have the word **surprise.**
Who has the word that means almost the same thing as *superb*?

I have the word **superior.**
Who has the word that names the person who is someone's boss?

I have the word **supervisor.**
Who has the word that names the extra charge you
have to pay sometimes when you travel?

I have the word **surcharge.**
Who has the word that names the extra amount of jeans a
clothing store could be left with at the end of a season?

I have the word **surplus.**
Who has the meanings of the prefixes **sur-** and **super-?**

I have **over, above,** or **beyond.**
Who has the word that describes a fabulous piece of writing?

I have the word **superb.**
Who has the first card?

Vocabulary Quiz: super-, sur-

Shade in the bubble for the correct word.

Ⓐ Ⓑ Ⓒ Ⓓ   **1.** What person would be employed as the head of a school district?
  A) superior   **B)** superintendent   **C)** surreal   **D)** superb

Ⓐ Ⓑ Ⓒ Ⓓ   **2.** When you combine and layer two pictures taken on a digital camera what are you doing?
  A) surprising   **B)** superimposing   **C)** surtaxing   **D)** surcharging

Ⓐ Ⓑ Ⓒ Ⓓ   **3.** His score on the test for chapter 5 was _____ to his score on the chapter 4 test.
  A) superimposed   **B)** superior   **C)** supervisor   **D)** surreal

Ⓐ Ⓑ Ⓒ Ⓓ   **4.** What type of artwork could include images that are life sized and miniature?
  A) surreal   **B)** superior   **C)** superb   **D)** superimposed

Ⓐ Ⓑ Ⓒ Ⓓ   **5.** The airline added a _____ of $10 for luggage that weighed over 50 pounds.
  A) surtax   **B)** surcharge   **C)** supervisor   **D)** surprise

Ⓐ Ⓑ Ⓒ Ⓓ   **6.** If you don't like the service you get, whom do you ask to speak with?
  A) subordinate   **B)** surpriser   **C)** surcharger   **D)** supervisor

Ⓐ Ⓑ Ⓒ Ⓓ   **7.** Some products are sold with this extra tax added.
  A) surcharge   **B)** superior   **C)** superintendent   **D)** surtax

Ⓐ Ⓑ Ⓒ Ⓓ   **8.** Wow! It was certainly a _____ when the refund check arrived!
  A) surcharge   **B)** supervise   **C)** surprise   **D)** superb

Ⓐ Ⓑ Ⓒ Ⓓ   **9.** Your speech was simply _____!
  A) superb   **B)** subordinate   **C)** superimposed   **D)** surcharged

Ⓐ Ⓑ Ⓒ Ⓓ   **10.** When there is a _____ of goods, the price will go down because there are more goods than people need to buy.
  A) surcharge   **B)** surtax   **C)** superior   **D)** surplus

Write the correct word on the line so the sentence makes sense.

11. The store intercom announced, "We have a _____ of apples! You can now get ten for $1.00!"

12. A person who is a subordinate will work under some type of _____.

13. The girl and boy did a _____ job painting the outside of their tree house.

14. The _____ artwork was displayed at the museum.

15. Kevin was in a state of _____ when he came home to find the entire house cleaned.

Name _____   Date _____

Review Test: sub- and super-, sur-

Shade in the bubble for the correct word.

Ⓐ Ⓑ Ⓒ Ⓓ   **1.** I rode in a _____ and was able to view all sorts of sea life without even getting wet.
A) subway   **B)** surprise   **C)** submarine   **D)** supervisor

Ⓐ Ⓑ Ⓒ Ⓓ   **2.** This is a person who manages others in a company.
A) subordinate   **B)** supervisor   **C)** superior   **D)** subcutaneous

Ⓐ Ⓑ Ⓒ Ⓓ   **3.** When the girl in Tom Riche's Fan Club finally met him, she was so overly excited that she said the experience seemed _____.
A) subconscious   **B)** subjected   **C)** surreal   **D)** superimposed

Ⓐ Ⓑ Ⓒ Ⓓ   **4.** When you take a cruise, there is a _____ that pays for the ports at which you stop.
A) surcharge   **B)** surplus   **C)** surprise   **D)** surreal

Ⓐ Ⓑ Ⓒ Ⓓ   **5.** This is a system of pipes under the ground that supplies water to plants.
A) submerge   **B)** subirrigation **C)** superb   **D)** surreal

Ⓐ Ⓑ Ⓒ Ⓓ   **6.** They had a _____ of ornaments so the store put them on the clearance table.
A) submerge   **B)** surtax   **C)** surplus   **D)** superimposition

Ⓐ Ⓑ Ⓒ Ⓓ   **7.** While living at home with your parents, you will be _____ to the rules of their household.
A) superimposed   **B)** subdued   **C)** supervised   **D)** subjected

Ⓐ Ⓑ Ⓒ Ⓓ   **8.** When taking swimming lessons, the coach blew in the baby's face before the baby was gently _____ into the water to make sure he held his breath.
A) subdued   **B)** submarine   **C)** submerged   **D)** supervised

Ⓐ Ⓑ Ⓒ Ⓓ   **9.** Your _____ is where thoughts and actions go when you no longer need to actively think about them.
A) submarine   **B)** supervisor   **C)** subconscious   **D)** superimposed

Ⓐ Ⓑ Ⓒ Ⓓ   **10.** Mrs. Charlesworth's students felt her teaching style was _____ to the other teacher's style.
A) subfreezing   **B)** superimposed   **C)** superior   **D)** subcutaneous

Ⓐ Ⓑ Ⓒ Ⓓ   **11.** What does the prefix **sub-** mean?
A) under   **B)** over   **C)** beyond   **D)** better

Ⓐ Ⓑ Ⓒ Ⓓ   **12.** You will need to pack special equipment if you plan on spending your vacation in _____ temperatures.
A) subconscious   **B)** subfreezing   **C)** subordinate   **D)** supervised

Ⓐ Ⓑ Ⓒ Ⓓ   **13.** What does the prefix **super-** mean in the words *superimpose* and *supervisor*?
A) over   **B)** under   **C)** better   **D)** more

Ⓐ Ⓑ Ⓒ Ⓓ   **14.** You will find this type of passageway under the ground.
A) subway   **B)** subirrigate   **C)** superintendent   **D)** submerge

Ⓐ Ⓑ Ⓒ Ⓓ   **15.** The stinger left behind when Chris smacked the wasp was _____.
A) subdued   **B)** superimposed   **C)** superior   **D)** subcutaneous

Prefixes and Suffixes © 2004 Creative Teaching Press

Word List: un-

un-	not, none

Vocabulary	Definitions
uncertain (adj)	**not** sure
uncommon (adj)	rare; **not** the usual; remarkable
unconscious (adj)	**not** within thought; **not** awake
undecided (adj)	**not** yet at the point of making a decision
unexpected (adj)	**not** what someone thought would happen; **not** predicted
unmistakable (adj)	clear; can**not** be understood the wrong way; **not** able to be confused or misunderstood
unnecessary (adj)	**not** required
untidy (adj)	messy; **not** neat; **not** organized
unwise (adj)	**not** smart
unworthy (adj)	**not** deserving; **not** having any value

Vocabulary Sort: un-

uncertain	rare; **not** the usual; remarkable
unmistakable	**not** required
untidy	**not** what someone thought would happen; **not** predicted
unworthy	clear; can**not** be understood the wrong way; **not** able to be confused or misunderstood
undecided	**not** deserving; **not** having any value
unexpected	messy; **not** neat; **not** organized
unwise	**not** sure
unconscious	**not** smart
unnecessary	**not** within thought; **not** awake
uncommon	**not** yet at the point of making a decision

Prefixes and Suffixes © 2004 Creative Teaching Press

Read-Around Review: un-

I have the first card.
Who has the prefix that means **not?**

I have the prefix **un-.**
Who has the word that describes something that you don't have to do?

I have the word **unnecessary.**
Who has the word that describes when you are **not** sure what to do?

I have the word **uncertain.**
Who has the word that describes a choice that was **not** smart?

I have the word **unwise.**
Who has the word that describes something that is rare and few people have it?

I have the word **uncommon.**
Who has the word that describes a typical child's room before he or she is told to clean it?

I have the word **untidy.**
Who has the word that describes the state of mind you are in when you dream?

I have the word **unconscious.**
Who has the word that describes the point of thinking where you can't make a decision?

I have the word **undecided.**
Who has the word that describes something that happens that was a surprise?

I have the word **unexpected.**
Who has the word that describes someone who is **not** deserving of the rewards he or she received?

I have the word **unworthy.**
Who has the word that describes something that is clear and couldn't be confused with anything else?

I have the word **unmistakable.**
Who has the first card?

Name _____   Date _____

Vocabulary Quiz: un-

Shade in the bubble for the correct word.

Ⓐ Ⓑ Ⓒ Ⓓ   **1.** The jury could not decide. They were still trying to figure out the facts. What are they?
A) unmistakable   **B)** undecided   **C)** unrealistic   **D)** unexpected

Ⓐ Ⓑ Ⓒ Ⓓ   **2.** You usually dream while you are in which state?
A) unconscious   **B)** unexpected   **C)** unworthy   **D)** uncertain

Ⓐ Ⓑ Ⓒ Ⓓ   **3.** Chris did not deserve to join the class in the pizza party since he was teasing people on the playground every day. What was he?
A) untidy   **B)** unworthy   **C)** unmistakable   **D)** unequal

Ⓐ Ⓑ Ⓒ Ⓓ   **4.** Sophie used this word to describe Alex's room, which always had piles of clothes on the floor.
A) untidy   **B)** unnecessary   **C)** unconscious   **D)** uncertain

Ⓐ Ⓑ Ⓒ Ⓓ   **5.** A blue diamond is a very rare stone. What is it?
A) unworthy   **B)** unwise   **C)** unnecessary   **D)** uncommon

Ⓐ Ⓑ Ⓒ Ⓓ   **6.** Chloe doesn't know if she can handle the responsibility of a pet turtle yet. How does she feel?
A) untidy   **B)** uncertain   **C)** unmistakable   **D)** uncommon

Ⓐ Ⓑ Ⓒ Ⓓ   **7.** Which type of choice usually gets you in trouble?
A) unconscious   **B)** unworthy   **C)** unequal   **D)** unwise

Ⓐ Ⓑ Ⓒ Ⓓ   **8.** At the Spy Expo, Max saw the exact car that was in his favorite film. It was _____.
A) unmistakable   **B)** undecided   **C)** unconscious   **D)** untidy

Ⓐ Ⓑ Ⓒ Ⓓ   **9.** This is what a true random act of kindness will always be.
A) unworthy   **B)** unequal   **C)** unexpected   **D)** untidy

Ⓐ Ⓑ Ⓒ Ⓓ   **10.** Dave drove his motorcycle to the gas station. He discovered it was already full of gas. The trip to the gas station was _____.
A) unworthy   **B)** unnecessary   **C)** unconscious   **D)** untidy

Write the correct word on the line so the sentence makes sense.

11. Is your room usually clean and organized or does it get a bit _____?

12. The actor said, "Thank you so much for the award, but I am _____ of it. I just got lucky enough to have good actors to work with."

13. Your dreams take place in your _____ sleep.

14. That painting is _____! It is clearly a Van Gogh!

15. Taking the final math test was _____ since Erin got 100% on her pretest and on every quiz.

Word List: dis-

dis-	not, none

Vocabulary	Definitions
disadvantage (n)	an unfavorable situation that is **not** good
disagreement (n)	a quarrel; **not** able to come to an agreement; **not** of the same opinion
disappoint (v)	to let someone down; to **not** make someone proud or satisfied
discontinue (v)	to end something; to **not** use anymore; cease
dismal (adj)	**not** good; depressing; dreary; bleak
disobedient (adj)	**not** following the rules
disorganized (adj)	messy; **not** neat; **not** able to find things
disposable (adj)	**not** worthy of being kept; easily given or thrown away; able to be easily replaced
disrespectful (adj)	**not** polite; rude; **not** courteous
disturb (v)	to bother or pester; **not** leaving someone alone

Prefixes and Suffixes © 2004 Creative Teaching Press

Vocabulary Sort: dis-

disagreement	**not** following the rules
discontinue	**not** good; depressing; dreary; bleak
disorganized	**not** worthy of being kept; easily given or thrown away; able to be easily replaced
disadvantage	to let someone down; to **not** make someone proud or satisfied
disappoint	a quarrel; **not** able to come to an agreement; **not** of the same opinion
disturb	**not** polite; rude; **not** courteous
dismal	to bother or pester; **not** leaving someone alone
disposable	to end something; to **not** use anymore; cease
disobedient	an unfavorable situation that is **not** good
disrespectful	messy; **not** neat; **not** able to find things

Prefixes and Suffixes © 2004 Creative Teaching Press

Read-Around Review: dis-

I have the first card.
Who has the prefix that means **not?**

I have the prefix **dis-.**
Who has the word that describes a person's behavior when he or she is always
getting into trouble?

I have the word **disobedient.**
Who has the word that describes a child who constantly interrupts the teacher and never
raises his or her hand?

I have the word **disrespectful.**
Who has the word that describes things that are thrown away and replaced with new things?

I have the word **disposable.**
Who has the word that describes the weather when it is raining for two weeks in a row?

I have the word **dismal.**
Who has the word that describes an argument or time when you do **not** agree with someone?

I have the word **disagreement.**
Who has the word that describes a desk that has piles of papers all over
it and drawers stuffed with many types of items that are **not** related?

I have the word **disorganized.**
Who has the word that describes what you do to a membership
or subscription that you don't want to have anymore?

I have the word **discontinue.**
Who has the word that describes how you would feel if you were
counting on something to happen and it never did?

I have the word **disappointed.**
Who has the word that describes what a child does when he
taps his mother on the head in the middle of her nap?

I have the word **disturb.**
Who has the word that describes something that will work against you?

I have the word **disadvantage.**
Who has the first card?

Prefixes and Suffixes © 2004 Creative Teaching Press

Name _____   Date _____

Vocabulary Quiz: dis-

Shade in the bubble for the correct word.

Ⓐ Ⓑ Ⓒ Ⓓ   **1.** If you walk into Paige's room, you will find toys mixed up with books on the shelves and in drawers. There are even socks between the toys! What word describes her room?
A) dismal   B) disrespectful   C) discontinued   D) disorganized

Ⓐ Ⓑ Ⓒ Ⓓ   **2.** Do you have one of those cameras that can be thrown away after you get the film developed? What is it?
A) disorganized   B) disposable   C) discontinued   D) disturbed

Ⓐ Ⓑ Ⓒ Ⓓ   **3.** A child who talks while others are talking is often not liked. What is this child?
A) disrespectful   B) disappointed   C) discontinued   D) disagreeing

Ⓐ Ⓑ Ⓒ Ⓓ   **4.** Brenton and Robert were told not to cross the street. Brenton listened. Robert didn't listen. What was Robert?
A) disrespectful   B) disobedient   C) disappointed   D) dismal

Ⓐ Ⓑ Ⓒ Ⓓ   **5.** If you decide you no longer want to watch so much TV, you might _____ your cable service.
A) discontinue   B) disobey   C) disrespect   D) disorganize

Ⓐ Ⓑ Ⓒ Ⓓ   **6.** It's always best to knock before entering a room. Otherwise, you might _____ someone.
A) discontinue   B) disadvantage   C) dismal   D) disturb

Ⓐ Ⓑ Ⓒ Ⓓ   **7.** If your uncle asks you to clean your room and you don't, what will you do to your uncle?
A) disappoint   B) dismal   C) discontinue   D) disagree

Ⓐ Ⓑ Ⓒ Ⓓ   **8.** When the clouds close in and the sky becomes dark, how do we describe the weather?
A) disorganized   B) disagreeing   C) discontinued   D) dismal

Ⓐ Ⓑ Ⓒ Ⓓ   **9.** Dawn wants to buy a house up north. Gerald wants to buy one down south. What are they in?
A) dismal   B) disagreement   C) disadvantage   D) discontinued

Ⓐ Ⓑ Ⓒ Ⓓ   **10.** When you want to bite into a big, juicy apple but you wear braces, what do you have?
A) a disadvantage   B) dismal   C) a disagreement   D) disposable

Write the correct word on the line so the sentence makes sense.

11. Becky is allergic to the medicine, so she must _____ taking it.

12. It was a _____ day, since everything seemed to go wrong.

13. Try not to be _____ to your classmates by making silly sounds.

14. If a student is very _____, she might be sent to the principal's office.

15. Having poor eyesight is a _____ when you are trying to read street signs.

Prefixes and Suffixes © 2004 Creative Teaching Press

Name _____ Date _____

Review Test: un- and dis-

Shade in the bubble for the correct word.

Ⓐ Ⓑ Ⓒ Ⓓ   **1.** Finish this analogy: neat : untidy : : smart : _____
     A) clever   **B)** unworthy   **C)** dismal   **D)** unwise

Ⓐ Ⓑ Ⓒ Ⓓ   **2.** Finish this analogy: help : assist : : _____ : _____
     A) discontinue : stop   **B)** start : discontinue
     C) go : discontinue   **D)** discontinue : go

Ⓐ Ⓑ Ⓒ Ⓓ   **3.** Monica and Lauren are best friends. Monica wants to play on the swings, but Lauren wants them to play handball together. What are they having?
     A) a disagreement   **B)** an unequal situation
     C) a disorganized game   **D)** a disadvantage

Ⓐ Ⓑ Ⓒ Ⓓ   **4.** Ms. RaeAnn, the school office organizer, received flowers. She didn't know why. What was the gift?
     A) disturbing   **B)** unexpected   **C)** untidy   **D)** unworthy

Ⓐ Ⓑ Ⓒ Ⓓ   **5.** People who don't know how to swim are at a _____ when staying at a hotel with a huge pool.
     A) disease   **B)** disadvantage   **C)** disrespectful   **D)** unequal

Ⓐ Ⓑ Ⓒ Ⓓ   **6.** The surgeon waited until the patient was _____ before beginning the surgery to remove his tonsils.
     A) unmistakable   **B)** uncertain   **C)** unconscious   **D)** disturbed

Ⓐ Ⓑ Ⓒ Ⓓ   **7.** If your notebook is _____, then you will have a hard time finding your study materials when you need them.
     A) unconscious   **B)** unattached   **C)** disorganized   **D)** dismal

Ⓐ Ⓑ Ⓒ Ⓓ   **8.** Some of the most common _____ products are diapers.
     A) unnecessary   **B)** unworthy   **C)** disappointing   **D)** disposable

Ⓐ Ⓑ Ⓒ Ⓓ   **9.** The class was _____ on whether they should have a pizza party or an ice cream float party.
     A) undecided   **B)** unmistakable   **C)** disrespectful   **D)** disappointed

Ⓐ Ⓑ Ⓒ Ⓓ   **10.** What does the prefix **dis-** mean?
     A) under   **B)** not   **C)** more   **D)** over

Ⓐ Ⓑ Ⓒ Ⓓ   **11.** The police officer was _____ whether the man was telling the truth or not.
     A) unavoidable   **B)** uncertain   **C)** disturbed   **D)** dismal

Ⓐ Ⓑ Ⓒ Ⓓ   **12.** You might _____ your family and yourself if you don't try your best.
     A) untidy   **B)** disappoint   **C)** disturb   **D)** discontinue

Ⓐ Ⓑ Ⓒ Ⓓ   **13.** When Mr. Beaudreau got home from work, he discovered that it was _____ for him to make dinner. His wife had already ordered pizza.
     A) unnecessary   **B)** disobedient   **C)** unmistakable   **D)** untidy

Ⓐ Ⓑ Ⓒ Ⓓ   **14.** The car is so _____ that there is a three-month waiting list to buy it.
     A) unconscious   **B)** dismal   **C)** unworthy   **D)** uncommon

Ⓐ Ⓑ Ⓒ Ⓓ   **15.** After finishing reading the book, the answer to the mystery was _____.
     A) unconscious   **B)** dismal   **C)** unworthy   **D)** unmistakable

Word List: inter-

inter-	between, among

Vocabulary	**Definitions**
interactive (adj)	involving people playing **among** themselves; an exchange of activity or information **between** people or people and a computer
interfere (v)	to get in **between** two people when it is not your problem or issue
interject (v)	to throw a remark into a conversation **between** two or more people
intermission (n)	the break **between** parts of a play, opera, or concert
international (adj)	**between** or **among** the nations of the world
Internet (n)	the worldwide computer system that allows communication and information sharing **among** people
interpersonal (adj)	**between** people (usually describing social activities)
interpreter (n)	a person who helps translate the languages **between** different people
interrupt (v)	to break into a conversation **between** people
interstate (adj)	**between** the states

Prefixes and Suffixes © 2004 Creative Teaching Press

Vocabulary Sort: inter-

Internet	a person who helps translate the languages **between** different people
interfere	to break into a conversation **between** people
intermission	to throw a remark into a conversation **between** two or more people
international	the break **between** parts of a play, opera, or concert
interject	to get in **between** two people when it is not your problem or issue
interrupt	involving people playing **among** themselves; an exchange of activity or information **between** people or people and a computer
interpersonal	the worldwide computer system that allows communication and information sharing **among** people
interstate	**between** or **among** the nations of the world
interpreter	**between** people (usually describing social activities)
interactive	**between** the states

Prefixes and Suffixes © 2004 Creative Teaching Press

Read-Around Review: inter-

I have the first card.
Who has the prefix that means **between?**

I have the prefix **inter-.**
Who has the word that describes what someone does when
he or she breaks into a conversation?

I have the word **interrupt.**
Who has the word that describes a game or an activity that
gets you involved with at least one other player?

I have the word **interactive.**
Who has the word that describes what you do when you throw
a comment or remark into someone's conversation?

I have the word **interject.**
Who has the word that describes the worldwide computer system of
sharing information **between** different people and companies?

I have the word **Internet.**
Who has the word that describes a freeway or highway that goes from one state to another?

I have the word **interstate.**
Who has the word that describes what someone does when he gets
in **between** two people and the situation doesn't concern him?

I have the word **interferes.**
Who has the word that names a person who helps translate two languages **between** people?

I have the word **interpreter.**
Who has the word that describes an activity that takes place **between** different people?

I have the word **interpersonal.**
Who has the word that names the stretch break **between** parts of a play or concert?

I have the word **intermission.**
Who has the word that describes sales, trade, or communication
between different nations around the world?

I have the word **international.**
Who has the first card?

Prefixes and Suffixes © 2004 Creative Teaching Press

Vocabulary Quiz: inter-

Shade in the bubble for the correct word.

Ⓐ Ⓑ Ⓒ Ⓓ   **1.** How are board and computer games described when they involve action and activity between people or a person and a computer?

        A) intercom   **B)** interactive   **C)** intermediate   **D)** intercostal

Ⓐ Ⓑ Ⓒ Ⓓ   **2.** "The first act of the play was amazing! I think I need a drink of water. I'll be right back." When did Joseph say this?

        A) intermission   **B)** interruption   **C)** Internet   **D)** interstate

Ⓐ Ⓑ Ⓒ Ⓓ   **3.** "I wish I knew what he was saying," said Erin. "I only speak English and he's speaking Spanish." What does Erin need?

        A) Internet   **B)** interruption   **C)** interpreter   **D)** intercom

Ⓐ Ⓑ Ⓒ Ⓓ   **4.** In the middle of the conversation between Mario and Zack, Jasmine came over and said, "Hey, that's not right!" What did Jasmine do?

        A) interject   **B)** Internet   **C)** interpersonal   **D)** intercoastal

Ⓐ Ⓑ Ⓒ Ⓓ   **5.** The business sells T-shirts to China, South Africa, and Canada. What type of business is it?

        A) interstate   **B)** interjected   **C)** international   **D)** interfere

Ⓐ Ⓑ Ⓒ Ⓓ   **6.** Two people are having a disagreement in the corner of the room. If you are smart, what will you **not** do?

        A) interstate   **B)** interactive   **C)** interfere   **D)** interpersonal

Ⓐ Ⓑ Ⓒ Ⓓ   **7.** What do you log on to in order to find information about bears?

        A) Internet   **B)** international   **C)** interstate   **D)** interjection

Ⓐ Ⓑ Ⓒ Ⓓ   **8.** Dane and Tyrone were talking about trains. Vincent came up and told them that he just got a new bike. What did Vincent do?

        A) interrupted   **B)** interpreted   **C)** interstated   **D)** interpersonal

Ⓐ Ⓑ Ⓒ Ⓓ   **9.** Luis drove on Highway 80, which led him from one state to another. What kind of highway was it?

        A) interstate   **B)** international   **C)** interpersonal   **D)** Internet

Ⓐ Ⓑ Ⓒ Ⓓ   **10.** Phuong likes helping people get along. What type of relationships does she like to be in?

        A) international   **B)** interpersonal   **C)** interstate   **D)** interrupted

Write the correct word on the line so the sentence makes sense.

11. The practice fire drill _____ what the class was learning.

12. The _____ computer game was so fun!

13. An _____ helps people who speak different languages understand each other.

14. People around the world share information on the _____.

15. During the _____ at the musical, people gathered around the booth that sold T-shirts and programs.

Word List: intra-

intra-	within, inside

Vocabulary	Definitions
intracellular (adj)	existing **within** the cells
intradermal (adj)	**within** the layers of the skin
intragalactic (adj)	**within** a galaxy
intramural (adj)	involving students from **within** the same school
intranasal (adj)	**within** the nose
intraocular (adj)	**within** the eye
intrapersonal (adj)	existing or occurring **within** your own mind
intrapsychic (adj)	**within** the mind
intrastate (adj)	**within** the state
intravenous (adj)	**within** the veins

Prefixes and Suffixes © 2004 Creative Teaching Press

Vocabulary Sort: intra-

intrastate	**within** the eye
intranasal	**within** the state
intrapersonal	existing **within** the cells
intradermal	existing or occurring **within** your own mind
intramural	involving students from **within** the same school
intravenous	**within** the layers of the skin
intragalactic	**within** the mind
intrapsychic	**within** the veins
intracellular	**within** a galaxy
intraocular	**within** the nose

Read-Around Review: intra-

I have the first card.
Who has the prefix that means **within?**

I have the prefix **intra-.**
Who has the word that describes something that occurs or exists **within** the nose?

I have the word **intranasal.**
Who has the word that describes something that occurs or exists **within** the eye?

I have the word **intraocular.**
Who has the word that describes something that exists or occurs **within** the layers of the skin?

I have the word **intradermal.**
Who has the word that describes sports that are played **within** the same school?

I have the word **intramural.**
Who has the word that describes something that exists or occurs **within** a state?

I have the word **intrastate.**
Who has the word that describes something that exists or occurs **within** the veins in your body?

I have the word **intravenous.**
Who has the word that describes anything **within** a galaxy?

I have the word **intragalactic.**
Who has the word that describes anything existing **within** the cells?

I have the word **intracellular.**
Who has the word that describes anything **within** the mind of a human?

I have the word **intrapsychic.**
Who has the word that describes anything that goes on **within** your own mind?

I have the word **intrapersonal.**
Who has the first card?

Name _____   Date _____

Vocabulary Quiz: intra-

Shade in the bubble for the correct word.

Ⓐ Ⓑ Ⓒ Ⓓ   **1.** If an eye doctor wanted to look within someone's eye, what kind of checkup would the doctor be giving?
  A) intranasal   **B)** intramural   **C)** intrapersonal   **D)** intraocular

Ⓐ Ⓑ Ⓒ Ⓓ   **2.** There are nine planets within the Milky Way. These are called what kind of planets?
  A) intraocular   **B)** intragalactic   **C)** intrapsychic   **D)** intradermal

Ⓐ Ⓑ Ⓒ Ⓓ   **3.** Which word could be used to describe the dreams that you have?
  A) intrapsychic   **B)** intranasal   **C)** intraocular   **D)** intradermal

Ⓐ Ⓑ Ⓒ Ⓓ   **4.** Some forms of transportation only work within the state. What are they described as?
  A) interstate   **B)** intrastate   **C)** intramural   **D)** international

Ⓐ Ⓑ Ⓒ Ⓓ   **5.** This type of needle will give medicine within the layers of the skin.
  A) intradermal   **B)** intrastate   **C)** intranasal   **D)** intracellular

Ⓐ Ⓑ Ⓒ Ⓓ   **6.** How could you describe a nose spray that helps you breathe?
  A) intranasal   **B)** intradermal   **C)** intramural   **D)** intracellular

Ⓐ Ⓑ Ⓒ Ⓓ   **7.** If a type of disease takes place within the cells, what could it be called?
  A) intradermal   **B)** intracellular   **C)** intramural   **D)** intranasal

Ⓐ Ⓑ Ⓒ Ⓓ   **8.** Which word describes sports or contests that take place within a school?
  A) intraocular   **B)** intramural   **C)** intrapersonal   **D)** intracellular

Ⓐ Ⓑ Ⓒ Ⓓ   **9.** Which word describes something that exists or occurs within your own mind?
  A) intrastate   **B)** intrapersonal   **C)** intranasal   **D)** internet

Ⓐ Ⓑ Ⓒ Ⓓ   **10.** When your doctor gives you a shot, it could be _____.
  A) intragalactic   **B)** intrapersonal   **C)** intramural   **D)** intravenous

Write the correct word on the line so the sentence makes sense.

11. Something within your eye is intraocular and something within your nose is _____.

12. When something is within the layers of your skin, it is called _____.

13. If the prefix **inter-** means *between* and **intra-** means *within*, then what do you think intermural sports are?

_____

14. Doctors throw away their _____ needles after each use for safety reasons.

15. To travel from one city to another city in the same state, you would use an _____ highway.

Review Test: inter- and intra-

Shade in the bubble for the correct word.

Ⓐ Ⓑ Ⓒ Ⓓ **1.** Finish this analogy: intrastate : interstate :: _____ : _____
   A) between : within   **B)** within : between
   C) together : apart   **D)** into : out of

Ⓐ Ⓑ Ⓒ Ⓓ **2.** Pauli has to have intraocular surgery. Where will the doctor operate?
   A) within her nose   **B)** between the layers of her skin
   C) within her veins   **D)** within her eye

Ⓐ Ⓑ Ⓒ Ⓓ **3.** Jasmine and LaTeisha were having a disagreement on the playground. Danielle came in and told Jasmine what she did wrong. What did Danielle do?
   A) interfered   **B)** used her intrapsychic abilities
   C) intrapersonal   **D)** used an interpreter

Ⓐ Ⓑ Ⓒ Ⓓ **4.** Dr. Roberts had his name legally changed to Dr. Nose. Why would he do this?
   A) He is an intraocular surgeon.   **B)** He is an intravenous surgeon.
   C) He is an intranasal surgeon.   **D)** He is an intradermal surgeon.

Ⓐ Ⓑ Ⓒ Ⓓ **5.** Tran's mom was on the phone with his teacher. He picked up the other line and made an excuse for his poor behavior that day. What did Tran do?
   A) interrupted   **B)** was intrapsychic
   C) got an interpreter   **D)** intermission

Ⓐ Ⓑ Ⓒ Ⓓ **6.** While going to college in the United States, Sukie needed one of these so she could understand what her professors were saying.
   A) Internet   **B)** interpreter   **C)** intrapsychic   **D)** intranasal

Ⓐ Ⓑ Ⓒ Ⓓ **7.** Sukie's favorite class was the one that taught her how to help people get along. What could the class have been called?
   A) international math   **B)** intrapsychic thinking
   C) intracellular diseases   **D)** interpersonal communication

Ⓐ Ⓑ Ⓒ Ⓓ **8.** While two students were discussing how to help the school raise money, another child walked over and said, "That's a silly idea!" What did she do?
   A) interjected   **B)** intrapersonal
   C) intercommunicated   **D)** used the Internet

Ⓐ Ⓑ Ⓒ Ⓓ **9.** Maria communicates with her friend, Sven, in Sweden. Sven communicates with his friend, Lars, in Germany. How might this happen?
   A) Internet   **B)** interpersonal speech
   C) intragalactic speech   **D)** intrapsychic thinking

Ⓐ Ⓑ Ⓒ Ⓓ **10.** What does the prefix **inter-** mean?
   A) under   **B)** not   **C)** between   **D)** within

Ⓐ Ⓑ Ⓒ Ⓓ **11.** What does the prefix **intra-** mean?
   A) under   **B)** not   **C)** between   **D)** within

Ⓐ Ⓑ Ⓒ Ⓓ **12.** At what time do the actors in a theater production take a little break and/or change the scenery?
   A) interruption   **B)** intermission
   C) intragalactic time   **D)** intramural

Ⓐ Ⓑ Ⓒ Ⓓ **13.** What does **dermal** most likely relate to in the word *intradermal*?
   A) veins   **B)** body   **C)** skin   **D)** cells

Ⓐ Ⓑ Ⓒ Ⓓ **14.** What does **psychic** most likely relate to in the word *intrapsychic*?
   A) mind   **B)** person   **C)** machine   **D)** cells

Ⓐ Ⓑ Ⓒ Ⓓ **15.** Phil owns a business that sells metal to other businesses in China, Mexico, and Australia. What kind of business is it?
   A) international   **B)** intrapersonal   **C)** interactive   **D)** intramural

Prefixes and Suffixes © 2004 Creative Teaching Press

Word List: circ-, circum-

circ-, circum-	round, around

Vocabulary	Definitions
circle (n)	a **round** shape that has no beginning or end
circlet (n)	a small circle; a ring or **round** band worn as an ornament, especially on the head
circuit (n)	a path for an electrical current to flow **around**
circulate (v)	to move **around** an area or a place, often returning to a starting point
circumference (n)	the distance all the way **around** a circle
circumflex (adj)	bending **around;** curved
circumnavigate (v)	to go completely **around**
circumrotate (v)	to turn **around** like a wheel
circumspect (adj)	careful; careful to look all **around** before doing something
circumvent (v)	to prevent something from happening by careful thinking; to get **around** something; to entrap

Vocabulary Sort: circ-, circum-

circumference	to prevent something from happening by careful thinking; to get **around** something; to entrap
circuit	careful; careful to look all **around** before doing something
circumspect	to move **around** an area or a place, often returning to a starting point
circulate	the distance all the way **around** a circle
circumnavigate	a small circle; a ring or **round** band worn as an ornament, especially on the head
circlet	bending **around;** curved
circumvent	to turn **around** like a wheel
circumflex	a **round** shape that has no beginning or end
circumrotate	to go completely **around**
circle	a path for an electrical current to flow **around**

Prefixes and Suffixes © 2004 Creative Teaching Press

Read-Around Review: circ-, circum-

I have the first card.
Who has the prefixes that mean **around?**

I have the prefixes **circ-** and **circum-**.
Who has the word that describes what you do when you are careful to look all **around**
before doing something?

I have the word **circumspect.**
Who has the word that names the distance all the way **around** a circle or circular object?

I have the word **circumference.**
Who has the word that names the **round** shape that has no beginning or end?

I have the word **circle.**
Who has the word that describes what sailors and explorers do when they travel
around the globe?

I have the word **circumnavigate.**
Who has the word that describes what you do to tires that spin **around?**

I have the word **circumrotate.**
Who has the word that means that you get **around** something or prevent it from happening?

I have the word **circumvent.**
Who has the word that describes a small circle that is often
a hair decoration worn **around** the top of the head?

I have the word **circlet.**
Who has the word that names the path through which electricity flows?

I have the word **circuit.**
Who has the word that describes how something is curved?

I have the word **circumflex.**
Who has the word that describes how a teacher might move around the room during a test?

I have the word **circulate.**
Who has the first card?

Name _____   Date _____

Vocabulary Quiz: circ-, circum-

Shade in the bubble for the correct word.

Ⓐ Ⓑ Ⓒ Ⓓ   **1.** When blood flows through your veins, it is doing this.
    A) circumflexing   **B)** circumventing   **C)** making a circuit   **D)** circulating

Ⓐ Ⓑ Ⓒ Ⓓ   **2.** When you go on a trip, you may do this.
    A) circumspect   **B)** circumnavigate   **C)** make a circuit   **D)** circumvent

Ⓐ Ⓑ Ⓒ Ⓓ   **3.** What does electricity flow through?
    A) circuit   **B)** circlet   **C)** circumference   **D)** circles

Ⓐ Ⓑ Ⓒ Ⓓ   **4.** If someone is wearing a circular band of flowers on her head, what might it be called?
    A) circumference   **B)** circuit   **C)** circlet   **D)** circumflex

Ⓐ Ⓑ Ⓒ Ⓓ   **5.** Name the shape that keeps going around and around without ending.
    A) circumference   **B)** circlet   **C)** circuit   **D)** circle

Ⓐ Ⓑ Ⓒ Ⓓ   **6.** If you sail around the world in 80 days, you have _____ the globe.
    A) circumnavigated   **B)** make a circuit
    C) circumvented   **D)** circulated

Ⓐ Ⓑ Ⓒ Ⓓ   **7.** What can you do to almost any bad situation by thinking before doing something?
    A) circumnavigate   **B)** circumrotate
    C) circumvent   **D)** get a circumference

Ⓐ Ⓑ Ⓒ Ⓓ   **8.** The mechanic will do this to the tires on a car.
    A) circumnavigate   **B)** circle   **C)** circumrotate   **D)** circumflex

Ⓐ Ⓑ Ⓒ Ⓓ   **9.** What do the prefixes **circ-** and **circum-** mean?
    A) into   **B)** around   **C)** through   **D)** bend

Ⓐ Ⓑ Ⓒ Ⓓ   **10.** What does circumference measure?
    A) distance across the middle of a circle   **B)** size of a circle
    C) distance around the outside of a circle   **D)** half of the inside of a circle

Write the correct word on the line so the sentence makes sense.

11. Finish this analogy: rectangle : circle :: perimeter : _____.

12. You can _____ getting wet in a rainstorm, even without an umbrella, with some clever thinking.

13. If a pilot plans to circumnavigate the United States in his plane, what will he do?
_____

14. Name three circular objects: _____ _____ _____

15. Write the word *circumflex* with the correct syllable breaks. _____

Word List: trans-

trans-	across, through

Vocabulary	Definitions
transatlantic (adj)	**across** the Atlantic Ocean
transcontinental (adj)	**across** a continent
transcribe (v)	to write **across** languages; to translate
transect (v)	to cut **across** or divide by cutting
transfer (v)	to move from one place to another; to move **across** places
translate (v)	to cut **through** any language barrier by changing one language into another
translucent (adj)	clear; light can pass **through;** see **through** but not perfectly clear
transparent (adj)	perfectly clear; obvious; light shows clearly **through**
transpiration (n)	the process of giving off moisture **through** pores of skin or **through** the surface of leaves and plants
transport (v)	to carry from one place to another; to carry **through** an area

Vocabulary Sort: trans-

translate	the process of giving off moisture **through** pores of skin or **through** the surface of leaves and plants
transcribe	to move from one place to another; to move **across** places
transport	**across** a continent
transfer	clear; light can pass **through;** see **through** but not perfectly clear
transparent	to cut **across** or divide by cutting
transatlantic	**across** the Atlantic Ocean
translucent	to write **across** languages; to translate
transect	perfectly clear; obvious; light shows clearly **through**
transpiration	to cut **through** any language barrier by changing one language into another
transcontinental	to carry from one place to another; to carry **through** an area

Prefixes and Suffixes © 2004 Creative Teaching Press

Read-Around Review: trans-

I have the first card.
Who has the word that means perfectly clear?

I have the word **transparent.**
Who has the word that means to move something from
one place to another, such as a book or money?

I have the word **transfer.**
Who has the word that describes what you do when you write something
across a piece of paper instead of keeping it just as oral speech?

I have the word **transcribe.**
Who has the word that means to carry something from one place to another
like you would if you brought something home from a vacation?

I have the word **transport.**
Who has the word that describes what you do if you cut **across** a loaf of bread?

I have the word **transect.**
Who has the word that describes a train that goes **across** the continent of North America?

I have the word **transcontinental.**
Who has the word that describes a ship that travels **across** the
Atlantic Ocean to carry goods from one country to another?

I have the word **transatlantic.**
Who has the word that describes what you do when you turn what
you are thinking in English into Spanish when you speak?

I have the word **translate.**
Who has the word that describes the scientific process of
moisture leaving **through** the pores of plants and leaves?

I have the word **transpiration.**
Who has the word that describes frosted glass that can let light
through but you can't see perfectly **through** to the other side?

I have the word **translucent.**
Who has the prefix that means **through** or **across?**

I have the prefix **trans-.**
Who has the first card?

Name _____   Date _____

Vocabulary Quiz: trans-

Shade in the bubble for the correct word.

Ⓐ Ⓑ Ⓒ Ⓓ **1.** Which word names part of the plant growth cycle in which moisture escapes through the leaves of plants?
    A) transfer   **B)** transporting   **C)** transpiration   **D)** transcribing

Ⓐ Ⓑ Ⓒ Ⓓ **2.** Tommy had to switch schools. What did he do?
    A) transferred   **B)** transcribed   **C)** translated   **D)** transported

Ⓐ Ⓑ Ⓒ Ⓓ **3.** While visiting Japan, Matthew needed help understanding the language. His friend Ryan spoke Japanese. What did Ryan do for Matthew?
    A) transported   **B)** transferred   **C)** transcribed   **D)** translated

Ⓐ Ⓑ Ⓒ Ⓓ **4.** Using glass blocks in homes is popular, since people can't see in but the rooms are brighter. What are the glass blocks?
    A) transparent   **B)** translucent   **C)** transpiration   **D)** transported

Ⓐ Ⓑ Ⓒ Ⓓ **5.** Trucking companies are hired to do this with products so they can get from one city or state to another.
    A) translate   **B)** transcribe   **C)** transport   **D)** transect

Ⓐ Ⓑ Ⓒ Ⓓ **6.** The glass on an overhead projector has to be like this so that whatever is written can be clearly read.
    A) transparent   **B)** translucent   **C)** translated   **D)** transported

Ⓐ Ⓑ Ⓒ Ⓓ **7.** Sophie went on a transatlantic cruise with her family. Where did she go?
    A) across the continent   **B)** across the Pacific Ocean
    C) across the Atlantic Ocean   **D)** across the state lines

Ⓐ Ⓑ Ⓒ Ⓓ **8.** The Mississippi River can be considered this type of river, since it goes from the north to the south of North America.
    A) transatlantic   **B)** transparent   **C)** translucent   **D)** transcontinental

Ⓐ Ⓑ Ⓒ Ⓓ **9.** What does the prefix **trans-** mean?
    A) into   **B)** around   **C)** across   **D)** bend

Ⓐ Ⓑ Ⓒ Ⓓ **10.** A court reporter has to do this to what is heard in the courtroom.
    A) transport   **B)** transcribe   **C)** transfer   **D)** transect

Write the correct word on the line so the sentence makes sense.

11. The dust on Sydney's windows makes them seem _____ rather than perfectly clear.

12. When trying to save money, it is smart to _____ money to a savings account.

13. If you had a chance to go on a transcontinental train trip, what would you do and see?

_____

14. Name three vehicles that transport things from one place to another.

_____ _____ _____

15. Write the word *translation* with the correct syllable breaks. _____

Prefixes and Suffixes © 2004 Creative Teaching Press

Review Test: circ-, circum- and trans-

Shade in the bubble for the correct word.

Ⓐ Ⓑ Ⓒ Ⓓ   **1.** Finish this analogy: translate : language :: _____ : goods
   A) transect   **B)** circumrotate   **C)** circumflex   **D)** transport

Ⓐ Ⓑ Ⓒ Ⓓ   **2.** Will needs to change schools since his family is moving to a new city. He will need to
   _____.
   A) transfer   **B)** translate   **C)** circumnavigate   **D)** transect

Ⓐ Ⓑ Ⓒ Ⓓ   **3.** Lucy plans on visiting Italy over the summer. She is going to the book store to buy a book
   that will tell her how to change her English words into Italian. What does the book do?
   A) transfers   **B)** transports   **C)** transcribes   **D)** translates

Ⓐ Ⓑ Ⓒ Ⓓ   **4.** Joseph and Peter love to travel. They plan to sail all around the continent of Australia this
   winter. What will they do?
   A) transport   **B)** circumnavigate   **C)** circumspect   **D)** transcribe

Ⓐ Ⓑ Ⓒ Ⓓ   **5.** Miyuki made an ornament for her tree. She wants to add some lace around the outside of it.
   What should she figure out so she doesn't waste any lace?
   A) circumflex   **B)** circlet   **C)** circuit   **D)** circumference

Ⓐ Ⓑ Ⓒ Ⓓ   **6.** You can make one of these board games out of aluminum foil, wire, a tiny lightbulb, and a
   battery. The light will shine if you match up correct answers. What type of board is it, since an
   electrical current will flow around from the battery, through the foil, to the lightbulb?
   A) circlet   **B)** circuit   **C)** circle   **D)** circumvent

Ⓐ Ⓑ Ⓒ Ⓓ   **7.** Janet cut across the cake. What was this act considered?
   A) transecting   **B)** circumflexed   **C)** circumspected   **D)** translated

Ⓐ Ⓑ Ⓒ Ⓓ   **8.** Shoma and her family were just in time to board the cruise ship that was sailing from Florida
   to Europe. What type of cruise was it?
   A) transcontinental   **B)** circumnavigated   **C)** transatlantic   **D)** transport

Ⓐ Ⓑ Ⓒ Ⓓ   **9.** In science class, the students were going to dissect a squid. They were told to carefully cut
   across the squid from the top to the bottom. What did they do to the squid?
   A) transect   **B)** transcribe   **C)** circumflex   **D)** circumrotate

Ⓐ Ⓑ Ⓒ Ⓓ   **10.** What does the prefix **circum-** mean?
   A) around   **B)** through   **C)** across   **D)** between

Ⓐ Ⓑ Ⓒ Ⓓ   **11.** What does the prefix **trans-** mean?
   A) across   **B)** round   **C)** around   **D)** together

Ⓐ Ⓑ Ⓒ Ⓓ   **12.** The huge diamond in the ring was almost clear enough to see through to the other side.
   What was the diamond?
   A) transparent   **B)** translucent   **C)** circumflexed   **D)** a circlet

Ⓐ Ⓑ Ⓒ Ⓓ   **13.** What does **scribe** most likely mean in the word *transcribe*?
   A) person   **B)** reading   **C)** writing   **D)** language

Ⓐ Ⓑ Ⓒ Ⓓ   **14.** What does **spect** most likely mean in the word *circumspection*?
   A) mind   **B)** looking   **C)** brains   **D)** school

Ⓐ Ⓑ Ⓒ Ⓓ   **15.** The Amtrak train system is an example of what type of railroad?
   A) translucent   **B)** circumnavigation   **C)** transcontinental   **D)** circumvented

Word List: mal-

mal-	bad or badly, wrong, ill

Vocabulary	Definitions
malady (n)	a sickness or illness; **bad** health
malefactor (n)	a person who does the **wrong** thing; an evil person
malevolent (adj)	wishing evil or **bad** will for others; mean
malfeasance (n)	**bad** conduct or **wrong**doing by a public official
malfunction (v)	to function imperfectly or **badly;** fail to operate normally
malice (n)	a desire to do something **bad** to someone else; doing something that is **wrong** on purpose
malignant (adj)	very **bad** or harmful; likely to cause death
malnutrition (n)	a poor diet; **bad** eating habits that result in poor health
malodorous (adj)	stinky; having a **bad** smell
malpractice (n)	an instance of **bad** conduct or treatment from a doctor or other professional

Prefixes and Suffixes © 2004 Creative Teaching Press

Vocabulary Sort: mal-

malice	an instance of **bad** conduct or treatment from a doctor or other professional
malefactor	a desire to do something **bad** to someone else; doing something that is **wrong** on purpose
malevolent	a sickness or illness; **bad** health
malnutrition	stinky; having a **bad** smell
malodorous	wishing evil or **bad** will for others; mean
malfunction	very **bad** or harmful; likely to cause death
malfeasance	a poor diet; **bad** eating habits that result in poor health
malady	a person who does the **wrong** thing; an evil person
malignant	**bad** conduct or **wrong**doing by a public official
malpractice	to function imperfectly or **badly;** fail to operate normally

Read-Around Review: mal-

I have the first card.
Who has the word that describes a person who wishes **bad** things to happen to other people?

I have the word **malevolent.**
Who has the word that describes what you will suffer from if you don't eat healthy foods?

I have the word **malnutrition.**
Who has the word that describes an awful smell or odor?

I have the word **malodorous.**
Who has the word that means a sickness or illness that might lead you to seeing a doctor?

I have the word **malady.**
Who has the word that describes a mistake a doctor carelessly made?

I have the word **malpractice.**
Who has the word that describes **bad** behavior by a mayor or senator?

I have the word **malfeasance.**
Who has the word that names what happens when a car functions **badly?**

I have the word **malfunction.**
Who has the word that describes something that is so harmful that it could be deadly?

I have the word **malignant.**
Who has the word that names a person who does the **wrong** thing,
makes **bad** choices, and is an evil character in a book?

I have the word **malefactor.**
Who has the word that names the desire to do something **bad** to someone else on purpose?

I have the word **malice.**
Who has the prefix that means **bad** or **wrong?**

I have the prefix **mal-.**
Who has the first card?

Prefixes and Suffixes © 2004 Creative Teaching Press

Name _____   Date _____

Vocabulary Quiz: mal-

Shade in the bubble for the correct word.

Ⓐ Ⓑ Ⓒ Ⓓ   **1.** Which word describes something that could lead to a recall (firing) of a state congressman?
     A) malignant   **B)** malpractice   **C)** malfeasance   **D)** malodorous

Ⓐ Ⓑ Ⓒ Ⓓ   **2.** When the cable television no longer works, there may be a _____.
     A) malfeasance   **B)** malodorous   **C)** malady   **D)** malfunction

Ⓐ Ⓑ Ⓒ Ⓓ   **3.** If a room was very malodorous, what would you buy?
     A) wires   **B)** air fresheners   **C)** scissors   **D)** smelly socks

Ⓐ Ⓑ Ⓒ Ⓓ   **4.** Kendra chooses to eat grapes instead of cookies and watermelon instead of candy bars.
She probably will not suffer from _____.
     A) malnutrition   **B)** malady   **C)** malevolent   **D)** malice

Ⓐ Ⓑ Ⓒ Ⓓ   **5.** The character in the movie acted with _____ when he pushed the girl
into the puddle of water.
     A) malady   **B)** malice   **C)** malpractice   **D)** malfeasance

Ⓐ Ⓑ Ⓒ Ⓓ   **6.** "So Ms. Ling, what has brought you here today?" asked Dr. Vu. What will Ms. Ling describe?
     A) her malice   **B)** her malpractice   **C)** her malefactor   **D)** her malady

Ⓐ Ⓑ Ⓒ Ⓓ   **7.** The villain in the movie who does all the bad things is also known as the
_____.
     A) malice   **B)** malefactor   **C)** malady   **D)** malfunction

Ⓐ Ⓑ Ⓒ Ⓓ   **8.** How would you describe a person who wants everyone to get bad grades except
himself?
     A) malevolent   **B)** malady   **C)** malfeasant   **D)** malpractice

Ⓐ Ⓑ Ⓒ Ⓓ   **9.** What does the prefix **mal-** mean?
     A) good   **B)** bad   **C)** ugly   **D)** around

Ⓐ Ⓑ Ⓒ Ⓓ   **10.** The doctor was sued for _____ when he gave the wrong type of blood
to a patient.
     A) malfeasance   **B)** malady   **C)** malpractice   **D)** malevolence

Write the correct word on the line so the sentence makes sense.

11. The tumor was not _____, so the patient has a chance to live a long healthy life.

12. Eat your fruits and vegetables so you will not ever have to worry about _____.

13. The pig pen was very _____, so the children plugged their noses.

14. Name three things that could malfunction.

_____ _____ _____

15. When the ferris wheel had a _____, the riders had to get off.

Word List: mis-

mis-	bad or badly, wrong

Vocabulary	**Definitions**
misbehave (v)	to act out **badly** or in the **wrong** way
mischievous (adj)	tending to make minor **bad** choices; teasing; full of tricks; naughty
miserable (adj)	feeling **badly;** the condition of feeling unhappy
misfortune (n)	**bad** luck
misjudge (v)	to make a **wrong** or unfair decision about someone
mislead (v)	to guide someone into the **wrong** direction; to be a **bad** influence
misspell (v)	to spell a word the **wrong** way
mistake (n)	a **bad** or **wrong** decision; error
mistreat (v)	to treat someone **badly**
misunderstand (v)	to think the **wrong** thing about what was communicated

Prefixes and Suffixes © 2004 Creative Teaching Press

Vocabulary Sort: mis-

misfortune	to make a **wrong** or unfair decision about someone
misbehave	feeling **badly;** the condition of feeling unhappy
misjudge	**bad** luck
misspell	to spell a word the **wrong** way
mistreat	to act out **badly** or in the **wrong** way
mistake	tending to make minor **bad** choices; teasing; full of tricks; naughty
miserable	to think the **wrong** thing about what was communicated
misunderstand	to guide someone into the **wrong** direction; to be a **bad** influence
mislead	to treat someone **badly**
mischievous	a **bad** or **wrong** decision; error

Read-Around Review: mis-

I have the first card.
Who has the word that describes what you do when you spell a word **wrong?**

I have the word **misspell.**
Who has the word that describes a person who is a bit naughty,
makes a few poor choices, and plays tricks on people?

I have the word **mischievous.**
Who has the word that describes what you make when you do something **wrong** on accident?

I have the word **mistake.**
Who has the word that tells how you treat someone when
you hurt their feelings or do mean things to them?

I have the word **mistreat.**
Who has the word that describes what you do when you show **bad** behavior?

I have the word **misbehave.**
Who has the word that describes how someone feels if she is very sad?

I have the word **miserable.**
Who has the word that describes what you do when you think someone is one way,
but when you get to know the person better you realize that you were **wrong?**

I have the word **misjudge.**
Who has the word often used in stories to describe **bad** luck?

I have the word **misfortune.**
Who has the word that describes what good mystery writers do to throw you off the track?

I have the word **mislead.**
Who has the prefix that means **bad** or **badly?**

I have the prefix **mis-.**
Who has the word that describes what you do when you do the **wrong**
thing because you didn't understand what the directions meant?

I have the word **misunderstand.**
Who has the first card?

Prefixes and Suffixes © 2004 Creative Teaching Press

Name _____   Date _____

Vocabulary Quiz: mis-

Shade in the bubble for the correct word.

Ⓐ Ⓑ Ⓒ Ⓓ   **1.** A child who behaved like this could also be called "naughty."
      A) mischievously   **B)** misleading   **C)** mistreated   **D)** misunderstood

Ⓐ Ⓑ Ⓒ Ⓓ   **2.** If you decide who your friends are based on how they look, then you will often
      _____ who people really are.
      A) mischievous   **B)** mistreat   **C)** misjudge   **D)** mislead

Ⓐ Ⓑ Ⓒ Ⓓ   **3.** One Monday morning, Trixie spilled her hot chocolate, fell and cut her finger, then lost her
      homework. What was the day full of?
      A) misfortune   **B)** mistreatment   **C)** misunderstanding   **D)** misleading

Ⓐ Ⓑ Ⓒ Ⓓ   **4.** Carly was ignored by her friends for something they assumed she had done. How did
      she feel?
      A) mistreated   **B)** mislead   **C)** mischievous   **D)** mistaken

Ⓐ Ⓑ Ⓒ Ⓓ   **5.** When you forget to write the letter **e** at the end of the word *mistake,* what have you done
      to the word?
      A) misspell   **B)** mispronounce   **C)** misjudge   **D)** misunderstand

Ⓐ Ⓑ Ⓒ Ⓓ   **6.** These should always be thought of as learning opportunities.
      A) misjudgments   **B)** mistakes   **C)** misleads   **D)** misadventures

Ⓐ Ⓑ Ⓒ Ⓓ   **7.** Cheyenne is sick in bed with a head cold. How might she be feeling?
      A) misjudged   **B)** miserable   **C)** misunderstood   **D)** mistreated

Ⓐ Ⓑ Ⓒ Ⓓ   **8.** Roxy thought her mom told her the keys were by the drink, but she had really told Roxy
      they were by the sink. What happened?
      A) misadventure   **B)** mistreatment   **C)** misunderstanding   **D)** misjudged

Ⓐ Ⓑ Ⓒ Ⓓ   **9.** While on the trail, Callie thought she knew which way to turn. The hikers ended up lost.
      What did Callie do to them?
      A) mislead   **B)** misbehavior   **C)** mischievous   **D)** mistreat

Ⓐ Ⓑ Ⓒ Ⓓ   **10.** Children who do this are usually punished in school and at home.
      A) misbehave   **B)** misjudge   **C)** misinform   **D)** misunderstand

Write the correct word on the line so the sentence makes sense.

11. People who _____ animals should never be allowed to have pets.

12. "Did I _____ you, or did you say that we could go to lunch five minutes early?"

13. The tour guide checked the map so he wouldn't make a _____ and get us lost.

14. The little sister in the story was so _____ that she was always getting herself
into trouble.

15. What do you think the part **fortune** means in the word *misfortune*? _____

Prefixes and Suffixes © 2004 Creative Teaching Press

Name _____   Date _____

Review Test: mal- and mis-

Shade in the bubble for the correct word.

Ⓐ Ⓑ Ⓒ Ⓓ   **1.** Finish this analogy: fast : slow :: kind : _____
   A) misjudging   **B)** mischievous   **C)** malignant   **D)** malevolent

Ⓐ Ⓑ Ⓒ Ⓓ   **2.** Mayor Manchester was accused of _____ and removed from his job.
   A) misfortune   **B)** malfeasance   **C)** misspelling   **D)** malnutrition

Ⓐ Ⓑ Ⓒ Ⓓ   **3.** The repairman likes it when something has one of these so he can work and earn more money.
   A) malady   **B)** malpractice   **C)** misadventure   **D)** malfunction

Ⓐ Ⓑ Ⓒ Ⓓ   **4.** Dr. Shuman has to pay for insurance in case he is ever accused of this.
   A) a misunderstanding   **B)** malpractice   **C)** a malady   **D)** misadventure

Ⓐ Ⓑ Ⓒ Ⓓ   **5.** Kimberly tries not to pick her friends based on what they look like. She knows she might do what?
   A) misspell   **B)** misfortune   **C)** misjudge   **D)** mislead

Ⓐ Ⓑ Ⓒ Ⓓ   **6.** If you say you will do something without ever planning on doing it, what are doing to the person?
   A) malpractice   **B)** misjudging   **C)** malignant   **D)** misleading

Ⓐ Ⓑ Ⓒ Ⓓ   **7.** In most stories, there are good and bad characters. What could you call the bad characters?
   A) miserable   **B)** malefactors   **C)** malodorous   **D)** malignant

Ⓐ Ⓑ Ⓒ Ⓓ   **8.** After Kiley walked into the storage room, he drove straight to the store to buy air fresheners. What word describes the storage room?
   A) malodorous   **B)** misinformed   **C)** mistreated   **D)** malfunctioning

Ⓐ Ⓑ Ⓒ Ⓓ   **9.** In the story *Island of the Blue Dolphins,* Karana had many different bad things happen to her. What did she have?
   A) misfortune   **B)** malice   **C)** misunderstanding   **D)** malnutrition

Ⓐ Ⓑ Ⓒ Ⓓ   **10.** What does the prefix **mal-** mean?
   A) bad, wrong   **B)** through, across   **C)** between   **D)** within

Ⓐ Ⓑ Ⓒ Ⓓ   **11.** What does the prefix **mis-** mean?
   A) bad, badly, wrong   **B)** through, across   **C)** between   **D)** within

Ⓐ Ⓑ Ⓒ Ⓓ   **12.** What probably happens to a mischievous child often?
   A) gets vegetables for dinner   **B)** earns money for college
   C) gets in trouble   **D)** visits the doctor

Ⓐ Ⓑ Ⓒ Ⓓ   **13.** What does **judge** most likely relate to in the word *misjudge*?
   A) person   **B)** decide   **C)** help   **D)** explain

Ⓐ Ⓑ Ⓒ Ⓓ   **14.** Finish this analogy: thanked : help :: punished : _____.
   A) misunderstand   **B)** misbehave   **C)** misspell   **D)** malice

Ⓐ Ⓑ Ⓒ Ⓓ   **15.** It is wise to apologize and try to fix these whenever possible.
   A) mistakes   **B)** malnutritions   **C)** malignant   **D)** malefactors

Prefixes and Suffixes © 2004 Creative Teaching Press

Word List: re-

re-	again, back

Vocabulary	**Definitions**
recheck (v)	to look at something **again**
reclosable (adj)	able to be sealed or shut **again**
reelect (v)	to vote someone into office **again**
refund (n)	money that is given **back;** money that is yours **again**
reimburse (v)	to give money **back;** to pay **back**
remember (v)	to bring **back** to mind; to have in your thoughts **again**
renew (v)	to make something new **again**
repeat (v)	to say something **again**
respond (v)	to answer **back;** to talk **again**
revive (v)	to bring **back** to life; to be alive **again**

Vocabulary Sort: re-

refund	to say something **again**
revive	to look at something **again**
reelect	able to be sealed or shut **again**
renew	to answer **back;** to talk **again**
reclosable	to bring **back** to life; to be alive **again**
repeat	to bring **back** to mind; to have in your thoughts **again**
remember	to give money **back;** to pay **back**
recheck	to vote someone into office **again**
reimburse	to make something new **again**
respond	money that is given **back;** money that is yours **again**

98

Read-Around Review: re-

I have the first card.
Who has the word that describes what you do when you forget
something, but it suddenly pops **back** into your head?

I have the word **remember.**
Who has the word that describes something that can be made new **again?**

I have the word **renew.**
Who has the word that describes what a trained parrot will do when you speak?

I have the word **repeat.**
Who has the word that describes what voters can do if they like their governor?

I have the word **reelect.**
Who has the word that describes what you do when you answer your teacher's question?

I have the word **respond.**
Who has the word that describes what you can sometimes do to a droopy plant if you
add some water and fertilizer?

I have the word **revive.**
Who has the word that means you get some money **back,**
usually after you bought something?

I have the word **refund.**
Who has the word that describes what you do when you aren't sure
whether or not you locked your front door before going to bed?

I have the word **recheck.**
Who has the word that describes some plastic bags that
can be opened and closed many times?

I have the word **reclosable.**
Who has the word that describes what a friend will do when she gives
you **back** the five dollars that she borrowed from you last week?

I have the word **reimburse.**
Who has the prefix that means **again?**

I have the prefix **re-.**
Who has the first card?

Name _____   Date _____

Vocabulary Quiz: re-

Shade in the bubble for the correct word.

Ⓐ Ⓑ Ⓒ Ⓓ   **1.** Every four years there is a presidential election. If a president has only served once, then he
may try to be _____.
   A) repeated   **B)** reelected   **C)** reimbursed   **D)** remembered

Ⓐ Ⓑ Ⓒ Ⓓ   **2.** The teacher had to do this when Wally raised his hand and said, "What did you say?"
   A) reelect   **B)** recheck   **C)** reimburse   **D)** repeat

Ⓐ Ⓑ Ⓒ Ⓓ   **3.** When someone asks you a question, what is the polite thing to do?
   A) remember   **B)** revive   **C)** recheck   **D)** respond

Ⓐ Ⓑ Ⓒ Ⓓ   **4.** The local high school has decided to do this to an old play by changing some of the songs
and characters to make them more like the people of today.
   A) revive   **B)** remember   **C)** recheck   **D)** repeat

Ⓐ Ⓑ Ⓒ Ⓓ   **5.** It is always nice when you _____ someone's birthday and other
important dates.
   A) revive   **B)** renew   **C)** recheck   **D)** remember

Ⓐ Ⓑ Ⓒ Ⓓ   **6.** If your mom realizes she doesn't have any cash to pay the gardener, then borrows yours with
the agreement to pay it back next week, what will she do for you?
   A) reimburse   **B)** recheck   **C)** reelect   **D)** respond

Ⓐ Ⓑ Ⓒ Ⓓ   **7.** The new washer and dryer cost $895.00, but if the buyer sends in the proof of purchase the
company will send $50.00 back. What will the buyer get?
   A) a repetition   **B)** a refund   **C)** repeated   **D)** reelected

Ⓐ Ⓑ Ⓒ Ⓓ   **8.** Many people use plastic bags for different purposes because the bags have this feature.
   A) reclosable   **B)** renewable   **C)** refundable   **D)** repeatable

Ⓐ Ⓑ Ⓒ Ⓓ   **9.** The leaves on the plant were drooping and turning yellow. What do you think Tom tried to
do to the plant?
   A) revive   **B)** recheck   **C)** remember   **D)** refund

Ⓐ Ⓑ Ⓒ Ⓓ   **10.** Peter enjoyed the magazine so much he wanted to _____ his subscription.
   A) renew   **B)** reimburse   **C)** reelect   **D)** refund

Write the correct word on the line so the sentence makes sense.

11. Since the mayor did a poor job, he will probably not get _____.

12. The Tidy Trashcan Company will _____ $10.00 to every customer who buys the Super
Deluxe Tin Trashcan by the end of the month.

13. Sarah wanted to _____ the dog dish to be sure she left Daisy enough water in her bowl.

14. The zippered plastic bags are _____ and can be used again and again.

15. A respectful student will _____ in class by raising his or her hand.

Word List: sym-, syn-

sym-, syn-	together, same

Vocabulary	Definitions
symbiosis (n)	a relationship between two different organisms that live **together** and depend on each other
symmetry (n)	having the **same** shape, size, and position on both sides of a dividing line
sympathy (n)	feeling kindness **together** with someone who suffers; pity; commiseration; compassion
symposium (n)	a conference or meeting **together** to discuss a topic
symptoms (n)	the conditions that **together** tell a doctor what is wrong
synagogue (n)	a place for meeting **together** for worship and religious instruction in the Jewish faith
syndicate (n)	a group of business people working **together**
synonym (n)	a word that has the **same** meaning as another word
synthesis (n)	parts put **together** to make a whole
synthetic (adj)	formed **together** from artificial parts; not genuine; fake

Vocabulary Sort: sym-, syn-

synonym	feeling kindness **together** with someone who suffers; pity; commiseration; compassion
syndicate	parts put **together** to make a whole
symptoms	having the **same** shape, size, and position on both sides of a dividing line
synthetic	a conference or meeting **together** to discuss a topic
synthesis	the conditions that **together** tell a doctor what is wrong
synagogue	formed **together** from artificial parts; not genuine; fake
symbiosis	a relationship between two different organisms that live **together** and depend on each other
sympathy	a word that has the **same** meaning as another word
symmetry	a group of business people working **together**
symposium	a place for meeting **together** for worship and religious instruction in the Jewish faith

Prefixes and Suffixes © 2004 Creative Teaching Press

Read-Around Review: sym-, syn-

I have the first card.
Who has the word that describes a group of people in the **same** business who work **together?**

I have the word **syndicate.**
Who has the word that describes a place where people meet **together**
to worship and receive instruction in the Jewish faith?

I have the word **synagogue.**
Who has the word that describes what a doctor is looking
for when he tries to make a diagnosis?

I have the word **symptoms.**
Who has the word that describes how some objects look
the **same** on both sides when divided down the middle?

I have the word **symmetry.**
Who has the word that describes a product that is fake
or created by putting artificial parts **together?**

I have the word **synthetic.**
Who has the word that means that parts were put **together** to make one whole object?

I have the word **synthesis.**
Who has the word that describes feeling kindness **together** with someone who suffers?

I have the word **sympathy.**
Who has the word that describes a word that means the **same** as another word?

I have the word **synonym.**
Who has the word that means a conference or gathering
at which people get **together** to discuss a topic?

I have the word **symposium.**
Who has the meaning of the prefixes **sym-** and **syn-?**

I have **together** or the **same.**
Who has the word that describes how two living things depend on each other?

I have the word **symbiosis.**
Who has the first card?

Prefixes and Suffixes © 2004 Creative Teaching Press

Name _____   Date _____

Vocabulary Quiz: sym-, syn-

Shade in the bubble for the correct word.

Ⓐ Ⓑ Ⓒ Ⓓ   **1.** This word describes something that is fake or created from artificial parts.
A) symmetry   **B)** symposium   **C)** symptoms   **D)** synthetic

Ⓐ Ⓑ Ⓒ Ⓓ   **2.** This word describes the relationship between two living things that depend on each other and live together.
A) symbiosis   **B)** syndicate   **C)** symposium   **D)** synonym

Ⓐ Ⓑ Ⓒ Ⓓ   **3.** This is when someone shows kindness toward someone who is suffering.
A) synthetic   **B)** sympathy   **C)** synagogue   **D)** symbiosis

Ⓐ Ⓑ Ⓒ Ⓓ   **4.** A conference or meeting together to discuss a topic is a _____.
A) symposium   **B)** syndicate   **C)** symbiosis   **D)** synthesis

Ⓐ Ⓑ Ⓒ Ⓓ   **5.** The doctor analyzes these to decide what is wrong with a patient.
A) symmetry   **B)** symptoms   **C)** symbiosis   **D)** synthetic

Ⓐ Ⓑ Ⓒ Ⓓ   **6.** This is a place where people of the Jewish faith meet to worship.
A) synthesis   **B)** symposium   **C)** syndicate   **D)** synagogue

Ⓐ Ⓑ Ⓒ Ⓓ   **7.** This word describes different parts put together to make a whole.
A) symmetry   **B)** syndicate   **C)** synthesis   **D)** symptoms

Ⓐ Ⓑ Ⓒ Ⓓ   **8.** A word that means nearly the same thing as another word is a _____.
A) synthetic   **B)** synonym   **C)** symposium   **D)** symbiosis

Ⓐ Ⓑ Ⓒ Ⓓ   **9.** An object has _____ when it is divided in half and both sides look identical.
A) symmetry   **B)** sympathy   **C)** synthesis   **D)** syndicate

Ⓐ Ⓑ Ⓒ Ⓓ   **10.** A group of business people working together is a _____.
A) syndicate   **B)** symbiosis   **C)** symptoms   **D)** synagogue

Write the correct word on the line so the sentence makes sense.

11. This triangle has _____ since I can draw a line down the middle and it's the same on both sides.

12. Today, my mom is at a _____ where the speakers are all talking about the stock market.

13. I had _____ for my friend who was suffering from the loss of her dog.

14. I know that the words *kind, nice,* and *friendly* are all _____.

15. Is your fur coat real or _____?

Prefixes and Suffixes © 2004 Creative Teaching Press

Review Test: re- and sym-, syn-

Shade in the bubble for the correct word.

Ⓐ Ⓑ Ⓒ Ⓓ   **1.** When taking any test, this is what you try to do to the information.
A) symbiosis   **B)** refund   **C)** remember   **D)** syndicate

Ⓐ Ⓑ Ⓒ Ⓓ   **2.** When Anna checked the label of her sweater, she was surprised to see that it was made out of this kind of material rather than natural wool.
A) synthetic   **B)** reimbursed   **C)** symbiosis   **D)** syndicate

Ⓐ Ⓑ Ⓒ Ⓓ   **3.** The author included her e-mail address on the back cover of the book. What was she hoping her readers would do?
A) respond   **B)** remember   **C)** syndicate   **D)** synthesis

Ⓐ Ⓑ Ⓒ Ⓓ   **4.** On medical television shows, you can often see doctors trying to do this to patients in the emergency room.
A) reimburse   **B)** refund   **C)** renew   **D)** revive

Ⓐ Ⓑ Ⓒ Ⓓ   **5.** If someone gives you an "IOU," what do they plan to do?
A) reimburse   **B)** renew   **C)** syndicate   **D)** recheck

Ⓐ Ⓑ Ⓒ Ⓓ   **6.** What word describes something that looks the same on both sides?
A) symmetrical   **B)** symbiosis   **C)** sympathy   **D)** repetition

Ⓐ Ⓑ Ⓒ Ⓓ   **7.** The words *kind, nice,* and *sweet* are all _____.
A) synthetic   **B)** repetition   **C)** synonyms   **D)** symbiosis

Ⓐ Ⓑ Ⓒ Ⓓ   **8.** When you feel kindness toward someone who is suffering, what are you showing?
A) symbiosis   **B)** sympathy   **C)** reimbursement   **D)** plantation

Ⓐ Ⓑ Ⓒ Ⓓ   **9.** When visiting the doctor, what will the doctor be looking for?
A) refunds   **B)** symptoms   **C)** reelection   **D)** synagogues

Ⓐ Ⓑ Ⓒ Ⓓ   **10.** What does the prefix **re-** mean?
A) again   **B)** through, across   **C)** between   **D)** together, same

Ⓐ Ⓑ Ⓒ Ⓓ   **11.** What do the prefixes **syn-** and **sym-** mean?
A) together, same   **B)** within   **C)** again   **D)** opposite

Ⓐ Ⓑ Ⓒ Ⓓ   **12.** What do you think people who go to a symposium do?
A) try different foods   **B)** get money back
C) put things together   **D)** learn new things

Ⓐ Ⓑ Ⓒ Ⓓ   **13.** What does **elect** most likely mean in the word *reelect*?
A) person   **B)** vote   **C)** earn   **D)** explain

Ⓐ Ⓑ Ⓒ Ⓓ   **14.** Finish this analogy: reelect : officers :: refund : _____
A) people   **B)** money   **C)** papers   **D)** plants

Ⓐ Ⓑ Ⓒ Ⓓ   **15.** Which of the following is probably not reclosable?
A) trashcans   **B)** cans of soup   **C)** water bottles   **D)** cereal boxes

Word List: hypo-

hypo-	under, below, less

Vocabulary	**Definitions**
hypoallergenic (adj)	**less** likely to cause allergies
hypocrisy (n)	the practice of being **less** than genuine; pretending to be someone you are not
hypodermic (adj)	**under** the skin
hypogeal (adj)	located **below** the surface of the ground
hypoglossal (adj)	**under** the tongue
hypoglycemia (n)	an abnormally low level of sugar in the blood; a blood sugar level **below** what is needed for healthy blood
hypotension (n)	having blood pressure **below** what is normal
hypothermia (n)	a temperature **below** the normal body temperature; low body heat
hypothesis (n)	an idea that is **under** investigation
hypothyroidism (n)	a disorder caused by a thyroid gland that is slower and **less** productive than normal

Prefixes and Suffixes © 2004 Creative Teaching Press

Vocabulary Sort: hypo-

hypothermia	located **below** the surface of the ground
hypodermic	the practice of being **less** than genuine; pretending to be someone you are not
hypoallergenic	**under** the tongue
hypogeal	an idea that is **under** investigation
hypotension	a temperature **below** the normal body temperature; low body heat
hypothesis	an abnormally **low** level of sugar in the blood; a blood sugar level **below** what is needed for healthy blood
hypoglycemia	**less** likely to cause allergies
hypocrisy	a disorder caused by a thyroid gland that is slower and **less** productive than normal
hypoglossal	**under** the skin
hypothyroidism	having blood pressure **below** what is normal

Prefixes and Suffixes © 2004 Creative Teaching Press

Read-Around Review: hypo-

I have the first card.
Who has the prefix that means **under, below,** or **less?**

I have the prefix **hypo-.**
Who has the word that describes anything that occurs **under** the tongue?

I have the word **hypoglossal.**
Who has the word that names a health problem due to **low** blood sugar?

I have the word **hypoglycemia.**
Who has the word that describes what is formed to help
answer a scientific question in an experiment?

I have the word **hypothesis.**
Who has the word that names a health disorder that is caused
by a thyroid gland that doesn't work as fast as it should?

I have the word **hypothyroidism.**
Who has the word that often describes the condition of someone who has
been rescued from being in cold ocean water for a long period of time?

I have the word **hypothermia.**
Who has the word that describes something that goes **under** the
skin (usually related to a type of needle when giving shots)?

I have the word **hypodermic.**
Who has the word that describes a situation in which a
person says one thing and does another?

I have the word **hypocrisy.**
Who has the word that is listed on most makeup product packages so the customers
don't have to worry about getting allergic reactions to the products?

I have the word **hypoallergenic.**
Who has the word that names the health problem that
results from having **low** blood pressure?

I have the word **hypotension.**
Who has the word that describes something that grows **under** the ground?

I have the word **hypogeal.**
Who has the first card?

Prefixes and Suffixes © 2004 Creative Teaching Press

Vocabulary Quiz: hypo-

Shade in the bubble for the correct word.

Ⓐ Ⓑ Ⓒ Ⓓ   **1.** The patient was taking blood pressure medicine to help with this health problem.
   A) hypothermia   **B)** hypoglycemia   **C)** hypocrisy   **D)** hypotension

Ⓐ Ⓑ Ⓒ Ⓓ   **2.** The child didn't drown in the river, but she did suffer from this temporary health problem because the water was so cold.
   A) hypothermia   **B)** hypothyroidism   **C)** hypotension   **D)** hypoglycemia

Ⓐ Ⓑ Ⓒ Ⓓ   **3.** What does the prefix **hypo-** mean?
   A) over   **B)** under   **C)** through   **D)** cold

Ⓐ Ⓑ Ⓒ Ⓓ   **4.** Most skin doctors say that you should only buy products that have this word written on the label.
   A) hypodermic   **B)** hypothermia   **C)** hypocrisy   **D)** hypoallergenic

Ⓐ Ⓑ Ⓒ Ⓓ   **5.** You are being a _____ when you say one thing and do the opposite.
   A) hypodermic   **B)** hypothermic   **C)** hypocrite   **D)** hypoglossal

Ⓐ Ⓑ Ⓒ Ⓓ   **6.** Nurses and doctors know that these needles can pass germs from one person to another if they are not thrown away.
   A) hypothermic   **B)** hypodermic   **C)** hypothesis   **D)** hypoallergenic

Ⓐ Ⓑ Ⓒ Ⓓ   **7.** The doctor told her that she had _____ since her thyroid gland was underactive.
   A) hypothermia   **B)** hypoallergenic   **C)** hypothyroidism   **D)** hypothesis

Ⓐ Ⓑ Ⓒ Ⓓ   **8.** Be sure to think of a _____ before starting the procedure of the experiment.
   A) hypodermic   **B)** hypothesis   **C)** hypoglossal   **D)** hypotension

Ⓐ Ⓑ Ⓒ Ⓓ   **9.** A peanut is this type of plant because it grows underground.
   A) hypogeal   **B)** hypoallergenic   **C)** hypothesis   **D)** hypoglossal

Ⓐ Ⓑ Ⓒ Ⓓ   **10.** When you are sick, you may use this type of thermometer.
   A) hypothesis   **B)** hypotension   **C)** hypoglossal   **D)** hypogeal

Write the correct word on the line so the sentence makes sense.

11. Her _____ was that if she put the stem into red water, then the flower would turn red.

12. The body will be in danger of _____ after an hour of exposure to icy cold water.

13. The doctor used a _____ needle to give the baby her shots.

14. People with _____ often feel like they need to snack during the day, since their bodies don't have as much sugar in their blood as other people.

15. Write the word *hypotension* with the correct syllable breaks. _____

Prefixes and Suffixes © 2004 Creative Teaching Press

Word List: hyper-

hyper-　　　　over, beyond, high

Vocabulary	Definitions
hyperactive (adj)	**overly** active; abnormally busy
hyperbole (n)	an **over**stated comment; exaggeration
hypercritical (adj)	**overly** critical; harsh in judgment; hard to please
hyperextend (v)	to injure a body part (e.g., knee, elbow) by bending it **beyond** how far it should normally bend
hyperglycemia (n)	abnormally **high** level of sugar in the blood; a blood sugar level above what is needed for healthy blood
hypersensitive (adj)	**overly** sensitive; sensitivity **beyond** what is normal
hypertension (n)	abnormally **high** blood pressure; having blood pressure **over** what is normal
hyperthermia (n)	very **high** fever; body temperature **over** and **above** what is normal and healthy
hyperthyroidism (n)	a disorder caused by a thyroid gland that is faster than normal and **overly** productive; results in a rapid pulse, nervousness, and loss of weight
hyperventilate (v)	to breathe rapidly and deeply; to breathe **beyond** normal or what is necessary

Vocabulary Sort: hyper-

hyperthermia	**overly** active; abnormally busy
hyperbole	**overly** critical; harsh in judgment; hard to please
hyperextend	very **high** fever; body temperature **over** and **above** what is normal and healthy
hypercritical	**overly** sensitive; sensitivity **beyond** what is normal
hypertension	abnormally **high** level of sugar in the blood; a blood sugar level above what is needed for healthy blood
hyperventilate	an **over**stated comment; exaggeration
hypersensitive	abnormally **high** blood pressure; having blood pressure **over** what is normal
hyperactive	a disorder caused by a thyroid gland that is faster than normal and **overly** productive; results in a rapid pulse, nervousness, and loss of weight
hyperglycemia	to injure a body part (e.g., knee, elbow) by bending it **beyond** how far it should normally bend
hyperthyroidism	to breathe rapidly and deeply; to breathe **beyond** normal or what is necessary

Read-Around Review: hyper-

I have the first card.
Who has the prefix that means **over, beyond,** or **high?**

I have the prefix **hyper-.**
Who has the word that describes a medical condition
in which there is too much sugar in the blood?

I have the word **hyperglycemia.**
Who has the word that names the condition in which a person's
body temperature is **higher** than it should be to be healthy?

I have the word **hyperthermia.**
Who has the word that describes how someone is when
they are very hard on you and criticize everything?

I have the word **hypercritical.**
Who has the word that describes a person who is a very fast mover,
keeps very busy, and is **more** active than most people?

I have the word **hyperactive.**
Who has the word that is a medical problem for some people, since
it is not healthy to have abnormally **high** blood pressure?

I have the word **hypertension.**
Who has the word that describes what someone could do to his
or her knee or elbow if it bends **beyond** its normal range?

I have the word **hyperextend.**
Who has the word that describes a person who is **overly** sensitive
and gets his or her feelings hurt more easily than most people?

I have the word **hypersensitive.**
Who has the word that describes an exaggeration or
overstated comment that is not realistic?

I have the word **hyperbole.**
Who has the word that names a disorder caused by a gland that produces
too much and causes a rapid pulse and nervous feelings?

I have the word **hyperthyroidism.**
Who has the word that describes what someone does when he or she breathes too quickly?

I have the word **hyperventilate.**
Who has the first card?

Prefixes and Suffixes © 2004 Creative Teaching Press

Name _____   Date _____

Vocabulary Quiz: hyper-

Shade in the bubble for the correct word.

Ⓐ Ⓑ Ⓒ Ⓓ   **1.** The saying "That music is so loud that you can hear it in the next city!" is an example of this figure of speech.
  A) hyperactive   **B)** hyperbole   **C)** hypercritical   **D)** hypertension

Ⓐ Ⓑ Ⓒ Ⓓ   **2.** The cartoon character just kept telling the goose what she was doing wrong. She never heard what she did right. Which word describes the cartoon character?
  A) hypertension   **B)** hyperactive   **C)** hypercritical   **D)** hyperextend

Ⓐ Ⓑ Ⓒ Ⓓ   **3.** The doctor told her to be careful that she doesn't do this to her knee in her yoga class.
  A) hyperextend   **B)** hypersensitive   **C)** hyperthermia   **D)** hyperactive

Ⓐ Ⓑ Ⓒ Ⓓ   **4.** What do you call the medical condition in which your blood has too much sugar?
  A) hyperthyroidism   **B)** hypertension   **C)** hyperglycemia   **D)** hypersensitive

Ⓐ Ⓑ Ⓒ Ⓓ   **5.** Marcus' mom worried that he might be _____ since he is always moving around, can't sit still, and loves to be busy.
  A) hyperthermic   **B)** hyperactive   **C)** hypersensitive   **D)** hyperbole

Ⓐ Ⓑ Ⓒ Ⓓ   **6.** Mrs. Lee went to the doctor because she was feeling nervous and losing weight quickly. What could she have had?
  A) hyperthyroidism   **B)** hypertension   **C)** hyperglycemia   **D)** hyperbole

Ⓐ Ⓑ Ⓒ Ⓓ   **7.** Someone suffering from a very high fever could end up with this dangerous medical condition.
  A) hyperthyroidism   **B)** hyperthermia   **C)** hyperbole   **D)** hypertension

Ⓐ Ⓑ Ⓒ Ⓓ   **8.** The doctor told Mr. Colby that his blood pressure was normal. He did not need to worry about this medical condition.
  A) hyperthyroidism   **B)** hypertension   **C)** hyperbole   **D)** hyperglycemia

Ⓐ Ⓑ Ⓒ Ⓓ   **9.** Poor Pham! Every time the teacher reminds her to raise her hand she cries! How would you describe Pham?
  A) hypersensitive   **B)** hypercritical   **C)** hyperactive   **D)** hyperbole

Ⓐ Ⓑ Ⓒ Ⓓ   **10.** After Barbara got scared, she felt faint because she was _____ and breathing too quickly.
  A) hyperextending   **B)** being hypercritical
  C) hyperventilating   **D)** saying a hyperbole

Write the correct word on the line so the sentence makes sense.

11. The doctor said, "Quick! Bring me some ice. She is suffering from _____!"

12. Mario was so _____ that he would cry whenever he missed an answer on a test.

13. People who are _____ usually have few friends since they judge everyone harshly.

14. Writing sounds more exciting when _____ is used well.

15. The little girl was so _____ that she couldn't sit still long enough to eat dinner with the family.

Review Test: hypo- and hyper-

Shade in the bubble for the correct word.

Ⓐ Ⓑ Ⓒ Ⓓ   1. Finish this analogy: over : under :: _____ : _____
  A) hyper : hypo   **B)** hypo : hyper   **C)** more : hyper   **D)** less : hypo

Ⓐ Ⓑ Ⓒ Ⓓ   2. This disorder is caused when your thyroid gland is more productive than normal.
  A) hypothyroidism   **B)** hypoglossal   **C)** hypertension   **D)** hyperthyroidism

Ⓐ Ⓑ Ⓒ Ⓓ   3. If someone uses a hypoglossal method of taking your temperature, where are they putting the thermometer?
  A) in your ear   **B)** on your forehead
  C) over your tongue   **D)** under your tongue

Ⓐ Ⓑ Ⓒ Ⓓ   4. You are a scientist. You are wondering what would happen if you mix two liquids together. You have an idea you want to try. What do you make first?
  A) hyperbole   **B)** hypocrisy   **C)** hypertension   **D)** hypothesis

Ⓐ Ⓑ Ⓒ Ⓓ   5. Salvador doesn't ever stretch the exact facts in his writing. What does he most likely **not** use?
  A) hypothyroidism   **B)** hyperbole   **C)** hypertension   **D)** hypocrisy

Ⓐ Ⓑ Ⓒ Ⓓ   6. Carmen's big brother was always putting her down. He made her feel like she couldn't do anything right because he was so _____.
  A) hypercritical   **B)** hypocritical   **C)** hypersensitive   **D)** hyposensitive

Ⓐ Ⓑ Ⓒ Ⓓ   7. The rescued diver was quickly wrapped in many heat blankets. He must have been suffering from _____.
  A) hypothermia   **B)** hypotension   **C)** hypertension   **D)** hyperthermia

Ⓐ Ⓑ Ⓒ Ⓓ   8. Patti is not the least bit _____. She can sit still and read a book for hours.
  A) hypersensitive   **B)** hypodermic   **C)** hyperactive   **D)** hypercritical

Ⓐ Ⓑ Ⓒ Ⓓ   9. People who suffer from _____ must take medicine to lower their blood pressure.
  A) hypotension   **B)** hypertension   **C)** hypoglycemia   **D)** hyperglycemia

Ⓐ Ⓑ Ⓒ Ⓓ   10. What does the prefix **hypo-** mean?
  A) under   **B)** over   **C)** within   **D)** better

Ⓐ Ⓑ Ⓒ Ⓓ   11. Most products say _____ so people with severe allergies won't have to worry about them getting worse.
  A) hyperallergenic   **B)** hypoallergenic   **C)** hypocritical   **D)** hypersensitive

Ⓐ Ⓑ Ⓒ Ⓓ   12. What does the prefix **hyper-** mean in the words *hyperthermia* and *hyperglycemia*?
  A) high   **B)** low   **C)** better   **D)** cold

Ⓐ Ⓑ Ⓒ Ⓓ   13. The doctor used a _____ needle to give Joaquin his shot.
  A) hyperdermic   **B)** hypodermic   **C)** hypertension   **D)** hypotension

Ⓐ Ⓑ Ⓒ Ⓓ   14. Katie cries over almost anything. She may be a bit _____.
  A) hyposensitive   **B)** hypocritical   **C)** hypertension   **D)** hypersensitive

Ⓐ Ⓑ Ⓒ Ⓓ   15. The ballet teacher was careful to give her students proper instruction to prevent them from _____ their knees while dancing.
  A) hyperventilating   **B)** hyperextending   **C)** hypothesizing   **D)** hyperthermia

Prefixes and Suffixes © 2004 Creative Teaching Press

Word List: -able

-able	able to be

Vocabulary	Definitions
acceptable (adj)	**able to be** received the way it is; worthy; satisfactory
detachable (adj)	**able to be** unfastened, taken apart, or separated
honorable (adj)	**able to be** a person of honor; worthy; of high rank; worthy of respect
imaginable (adj)	**able to be** imagined or thought of
laughable (adj)	**able to be** laughed at; amusing; funny
portable (adj)	**able to be** carried from one place to another
refundable (adj)	**able to** have money given back again
renewable (adj)	**able to be** created again
repairable (adj)	**able to be** fixed
washable (adj)	**able to be** laundered or washed

Prefixes and Suffixes © 2004 Creative Teaching Press

Vocabulary Sort: -able

portable	**able to be** imagined or thought of
refundable	**able to be** received the way it is; worthy; satisfactory
detachable	**able to be** laughed at; amusing; funny
renewable	**able to be** carried from one place to another
acceptable	**able to be** a person of honor; worthy; of high rank; worthy of respect
washable	**able to** have money given back again
laughable	**able to be** created again
imaginable	**able to be** fixed
honorable	**able to be** laundered or washed
repairable	**able to be** unfastened, taken apart, or separated

Prefixes and Suffixes © 2004 Creative Teaching Press

Read-Around Review: -able

I have the first card.
Who has the word that describes being **able to** get your money back?

I have the word **refundable.**
Who has the word that describes a person who is **able to**
receive respect and honor from others?

I have the word **honorable.**
Who has the word that describes something that can be fixed, such as a car engine?

I have the word **repairable.**
Who has the word that describes something that can be taken apart, removed, or separated?

I have the word **detachable.**
Who has the word that describes clothing that can go into the washing machine
without being damaged?

I have the word **washable.**
Who has the word that describes something that is possible in one's mind?

I have the word **imaginable.**
Who has the word that describes resources that can be created again?

I have the word **renewable.**
Who has the word that describes containers and other
items that can be carried from one place to another?

I have the word **portable.**
Who has the word that describes something that is so ridiculous that people laugh at it?

I have the word **laughable.**
Who has the suffix that means **able to be?**

I have the suffix **-able.**
Who has the word that describes something that is worthy or satisfactory?

I have the word **acceptable.**
Who has the first card?

Vocabulary Quiz: -able

Shade in the bubble for the correct word.

Ⓐ Ⓑ Ⓒ Ⓓ   **1.** Many stores have signs promising to give you your money back if the product you buy is not 100% what you expect. What is your purchase?
       A) portable   **B)** refundable   **C)** imaginable   **D)** washable

Ⓐ Ⓑ Ⓒ Ⓓ   **2.** Which word would describe a mouse for a laptop computer?
       A) washable   **B)** refundable   **C)** detachable   **D)** imaginable

Ⓐ Ⓑ Ⓒ Ⓓ   **3.** A creative writer thinks of ideas that could occur. What types of ideas are these?
       A) imaginable   **B)** repairable   **C)** honorable   **D)** portable

Ⓐ Ⓑ Ⓒ Ⓓ   **4.** Which word best describes the President of the United States?
       A) renewable   **B)** washable   **C)** portable   **D)** honorable

Ⓐ Ⓑ Ⓒ Ⓓ   **5.** Which word best describes a funny character that pokes fun of himself in a movie?
       A) honorable   **B)** laughable   **C)** imaginable   **D)** renewable

Ⓐ Ⓑ Ⓒ Ⓓ   **6.** The best selling computers are the ones that can be carried from one place to another, such as to the airport, the office, or the bedroom. What are these computers?
       A) refundable   **B)** portable   **C)** repairable   **D)** acceptable

Ⓐ Ⓑ Ⓒ Ⓓ   **7.** Nancy's cell phone isn't working anymore. She found out it can be easily fixed. What is her phone?
       A) renewable   **B)** repairable   **C)** imaginable   **D)** acceptable

Ⓐ Ⓑ Ⓒ Ⓓ   **8.** Which word describes clothing that does not need to go to the dry cleaners, since the washing machine will not ruin it?
       A) refundable   **B)** imaginable   **C)** repairable   **D)** washable

Ⓐ Ⓑ Ⓒ Ⓓ   **9.** Remember that your work should always be at least at this level.
       A) acceptable   **B)** resealable   **C)** detachable   **D)** honorable

Ⓐ Ⓑ Ⓒ Ⓓ   **10.** Solar energy is an example of _____ energy since it can be created again and again by the sun.
       A) resealable   **B)** liable   **C)** renewable   **D)** interchangeable

Write the correct word on the line so the sentence makes sense.

11. The coat came with a _____ fur lining so you could wear it comfortably in many kinds of weather.

12. The teacher said that the length of the paragraph was _____ .

13. A broken garbage disposal that can be fixed would be described as _____ .

14. The label on the shirt said, "_____ in cold water only."

15. Mrs. Junker carried her _____ file box home so she could grade the papers after dinner.

Prefixes and Suffixes © 2004 Creative Teaching Press

Word List: -less

-less   without

Vocabulary	Definitions
breathless (adj)	**without** breath; out of breath
effortless (adj)	**without** having to try; easy
fearless (adj)	**without** fear; not afraid
motionless (adj)	**without** movement; still
odorless (adj)	**without** a smell
penniless (adj)	**without** money; poor
reckless (adj)	**without** responsibility; careless
speechless (adj)	**without** speech; lack of words; quiet
tireless (adj)	**without** getting tired; persistent
worthless (adj)	**without** value; not worth anything

Vocabulary Sort: -less

worthless	**without** getting tired; persistent
effortless	**without** responsibility; careless
speechless	**without** fear; not afraid
penniless	**without** movement; still
breathless	**without** money; poor
reckless	**without** speech; lack of words; quiet
fearless	**without** breath; out of breath
motionless	**without** a smell
odorless	**without** having to try; easy
tireless	**without** value; not worth anything

Prefixes and Suffixes © 2004 Creative Teaching Press

Read-Around Review: -less

I have the first card.
Who has the word that describes a person who is willing to try anything and is rarely afraid?

I have the word **fearless.**
Who has the word that describes a person who has just finished running a marathon?

I have the word **breathless.**
Who has the word that describes a person who is so surprised
that he doesn't know what to say?

I have the word **speechless.**
Who has the word that describes something that has no value at all?

I have the word **worthless.**
Who has the word that describes something that has no smell at all?

I have the word **odorless.**
Who has the word that describes a flag outside of a house on a calm sunny day?

I have the word **motionless.**
Who has the word that describes a person who has lost all of his or her money?

I have the word **penniless.**
Who has the word that describes something that is so easy
for you that it doesn't take any thought to do it well?

I have the word **effortless.**
Who has the word that describes someone working hard all night long?

I have the word **tireless.**
Who has the suffix that means **without?**

I have the suffix **-less.**
Who has the word that describes a person who does whatever
she wants without thinking about the results of her actions?

I have the word **reckless.**
Who has the first card?

Name _____   Date _____

Vocabulary Quiz: -less

Shade in the bubble for the correct word.

Ⓐ Ⓑ Ⓒ Ⓓ   1. Trenton loves to read. To him, reading is easy, fun, and a pure pleasure. Which word describes how reading is to Trenton?
   A) effortless   **B)** speechless   **C)** penniless   **D)** reckless

Ⓐ Ⓑ Ⓒ Ⓓ   2. Frankie found a ring in the street. He took it to the jewelry store. He was disappointed. What was the ring?
   A) odorless   **B)** timeless   **C)** penniless   **D)** worthless

Ⓐ Ⓑ Ⓒ Ⓓ   3. This word describes how a sterile room might smell.
   A) odorless   **B)** worthless   **C)** reckless   **D)** effortless

Ⓐ Ⓑ Ⓒ Ⓓ   4. Pat was allergic to bees. She always stood like this when a bee was around with the hope that the bee would quickly fly away.
   A) reckless   **B)** odorless   **C)** motionless   **D)** speechless

Ⓐ Ⓑ Ⓒ Ⓓ   5. Latoya loves to go rock climbing, scuba diving, and skiing. What is she?
   A) odorless   **B)** fearless   **C)** penniless   **D)** speechless

Ⓐ Ⓑ Ⓒ Ⓓ   6. In the play, the main character grew up without any money, a home, or fancy clothing. What could she have been?
   A) reckless   **B)** breathless   **C)** penniless   **D)** motionless

Ⓐ Ⓑ Ⓒ Ⓓ   7. The actor at the ceremony was so shocked that he didn't know what to say. What was he?
   A) speechless   **B)** penniless   **C)** effortless   **D)** odorless

Ⓐ Ⓑ Ⓒ Ⓓ   8. Which word best describes a farmer who wakes up before sunrise, works hard on the farm all day, and doesn't stop until hours after dark?
   A) fearless   **B)** worthless   **C)** tireless   **D)** breathless

Ⓐ Ⓑ Ⓒ Ⓓ   9. Anyone who doesn't drive safely on the road will be described as this type of driver.
   A) penniless   **B)** worthless   **C)** effortless   **D)** reckless

Ⓐ Ⓑ Ⓒ Ⓓ   10. After swimming twenty laps across the pool, the swimmer felt _____.
   A) breathless   **B)** motionless   **C)** effortless   **D)** reckless

Write the correct word on the line so the sentence makes sense.

11. The liquid in the bottle was _____, but the smart girl knew it could be dangerous so she didn't drink it.

12. The _____ boy loved to climb trees although he knew he could easily hurt himself while doing it.

13. The man was _____ when he won the writing contest. He never even dreamed he would win!

14. The _____ worker began when the sun rose and worked hard until the sun set.

15. After her baby brother colored all over her stamp collection, she found out that the stamps were suddenly _____. She couldn't sell them for anything.

Review Test: -able and -less

Shade in the bubble for the correct word.

Ⓐ Ⓑ Ⓒ Ⓓ   **1.** Shellie was glad to find out that if the new pants didn't fit Christian, then her purchase would be _____.
   A) penniless   **B)** refundable   **C)** worthless   **D)** repairable

Ⓐ Ⓑ Ⓒ Ⓓ   **2.** Pedro got stage fright. He stood perfectly still when it was his turn to give his speech. Which word describes how he stood?
   A) motionless   **B)** laughable   **C)** detachable   **D)** breathless

Ⓐ Ⓑ Ⓒ Ⓓ   **3.** The main character in the movie made people giggle. This movie can be described as _____.
   A) effortless   **B)** imaginable   **C)** fearless   **D)** laughable

Ⓐ Ⓑ Ⓒ Ⓓ   **4.** Fred can carry his laptop computer anywhere he goes. What is it?
   A) timeless   **B)** portable   **C)** imaginable   **D)** worthless

Ⓐ Ⓑ Ⓒ Ⓓ   **5.** Which word describes a person who is worthy of getting an award for saving another person's life?
   A) worthless   **B)** renewable   **C)** honorable   **D)** reckless

Ⓐ Ⓑ Ⓒ Ⓓ   **6.** What do you call someone who does crazy things and takes risks without worrying about safety?
   A) effortless   **B)** reckless   **C)** renewable   **D)** repairable

Ⓐ Ⓑ Ⓒ Ⓓ   **7.** Mechanic Miguel said that the brakes could be fixed. What are they?
   A) worthless   **B)** effortless   **C)** repairable   **D)** laughable

Ⓐ Ⓑ Ⓒ Ⓓ   **8.** What type of effort is it when you try really hard time and time again until you succeed?
   A) washable   **B)** detachable   **C)** tireless   **D)** repairable

Ⓐ Ⓑ Ⓒ Ⓓ   **9.** Ashley just bought a new purse. The strap can come off or be left on so she can wear the purse over her shoulder. What is the strap?
   A) resealable   **B)** detachable   **C)** effortless   **D)** worthless

Ⓐ Ⓑ Ⓒ Ⓓ   **10.** What does the suffix **-less** mean?
   A) without   **B)** a person who   **C)** instead of   **D)** able to be

Ⓐ Ⓑ Ⓒ Ⓓ   **11.** What does the suffix **-able** mean?
   A) without   **B)** a person who   **C)** instead of   **D)** able to be

Ⓐ Ⓑ Ⓒ Ⓓ   **12.** If something is very easy for you, what would you call it?
   A) odorless   **B)** refundable   **C)** effortless   **D)** renewable

Ⓐ Ⓑ Ⓒ Ⓓ   **13.** What does **honor** most likely mean in the word *honorable*?
   A) worth   **B)** person   **C)** help   **D)** money

Ⓐ Ⓑ Ⓒ Ⓓ   **14.** What do you think the word *clueless* means?
   A) a part of a mystery   **B)** the answer to a riddle
   C) having no idea   **D)** out of energy

Ⓐ Ⓑ Ⓒ Ⓓ   **15.** At Pizza Palace, Chef Louie tries to make sure every worker is satisfied with how much money he or she makes. What do the workers think their pay is?
   A) worthless   **B)** penniless   **C)** imaginable   **D)** acceptable

Word List: -ology

-ology	study of

Vocabulary	**Definitions**
anthropology (n)	the **study of** humans
biology (n)	the **study of** life and living things
cardiology (n)	the **study of** the heart
dermatology (n)	the **study of** the skin
ecology (n)	the **study of** the environment
geology (n)	the **study of** the physical nature, structure, and history of the earth
graphology (n)	the **study of** handwriting and how it relates to a person's character
psychology (n)	the **study of** the mind
sociology (n)	the **study of** how people interact
zoology (n)	the **study of** animals

Vocabulary Sort: -ology

biology	the **study of** the heart
dermatology	the **study of** the physical nature, structure, and history of the earth
sociology	the **study of** the mind
graphology	the **study of** life and living things
zoology	the **study of** animals
anthropology	the **study of** how people interact
cardiology	the **study of** handwriting and how it relates to a person's character
psychology	the **study of** humans
geology	the **study of** the environment
ecology	the **study of** the skin

Prefixes and Suffixes © 2004 Creative Teaching Press

Read-Around Review: -ology

I have the first card.
Who has the name of the class you would take if you wanted to **study** the skin?

I have the word **dermatology.**
Who has the name of the class you would take if you wanted to **study** the heart?

I have the word **cardiology.**
Who has the name of the class you would take if you wanted
to **study** how people get along with each other?

I have the word **sociology.**
Who has the name of the class you would take if you wanted to **study** the environment?

I have the word **ecology.**
Who has the name of the class you would take if you wanted to **study** humans?

I have the word **anthropology.**
Who has the name of the class you would take if you wanted to **study** animals?

I have the word **zoology.**
Who has the name of the class you would take if you wanted to **study** life and living things?

I have the word **biology.**
Who has the name of the class you would take if you wanted to **study** the mind?

I have the word **psychology.**
Who has the name of the class you would take if you wanted to **study** a person's writing?

I have the word **graphology.**
Who has the suffix that means **the study of?**

I have the suffix **-ology.**
Who has the name of the class you would take if you
wanted to **study** the earth and its history?

I have the word **geology.**
Who has the first card?

Prefixes and Suffixes © 2004 Creative Teaching Press

Name _____   Date _____

Vocabulary Quiz: -ology

Shade in the bubble for the correct word.

Ⓐ Ⓑ Ⓒ Ⓓ   **1.** Brad loves nature and the environment. What might he study in college?
                A) ecology   **B)** biology   **C)** geology   **D)** zoology

Ⓐ Ⓑ Ⓒ Ⓓ   **2.** Rachel loves rocks, minerals, and gems. What might she study in college?
                A) geology   **B)** biology   **C)** sociology   **D)** anthropology

Ⓐ Ⓑ Ⓒ Ⓓ   **3.** Alyssa loves animals. What might she study in college?
                A) zoology   **B)** cardiology   **C)** geology   **D)** graphology

Ⓐ Ⓑ Ⓒ Ⓓ   **4.** Mr. Sharpee graduated from college with a degree that states he is an expert at analyzing a person's writing. He now works for the FBI. What does he specialize in?
                A) psychology   **B)** zoology   **C)** geology   **D)** graphology

Ⓐ Ⓑ Ⓒ Ⓓ   **5.** Dr. McDonald helps people who get rashes on their skin. What did he study in college?
                A) geology   **B)** biology   **C)** psychology   **D)** dermatology

Ⓐ Ⓑ Ⓒ Ⓓ   **6.** Sam's dad is a heart surgeon. Sam wants to be just like him. What should Sam plan to study in college?
                A) cardiology   **B)** dermatology   **C)** zoology   **D)** biology

Ⓐ Ⓑ Ⓒ Ⓓ   **7.** Dr. Olson enjoys studying ancient humans and how they have changed and adapted over the years. What was his college degree in?
                A) anthropology   **B)** psychology   **C)** geology   **D)** dermatology

Ⓐ Ⓑ Ⓒ Ⓓ   **8.** Bruce would get the "Mr. Friendly" award. He loves being with people. What would he enjoy the most in college?
                A) biology   **B)** sociology   **C)** zoology   **D)** psychology

Ⓐ Ⓑ Ⓒ Ⓓ   **9.** Danielle likes to study how living things survive. What might she enjoy studying in college?
                A) biology   **B)** dermatology   **C)** geology   **D)** cardiology

Ⓐ Ⓑ Ⓒ Ⓓ   **10.** Yasmine loves to figure things out. She likes to learn about the brain. What would she enjoy studying?
                A) graphology   **B)** anthropology   **C)** psychology   **D)** zoology

Finish each analogy.

11. graphology : writing :: _____ : environment

12. anthropology : humans :: zoology : _____

13. skin : _____ :: heart : cardiology

14. mind : heart :: _____ : cardiology

15. biology : living things :: _____ : rocks

Word List: -phobia

-phobia	fear of

Vocabulary	Definitions
ailurophobia (n)	**fear of** cats
arachnophobia (n)	**fear of** spiders
acrophobia (n)	**fear of** heights
graphophobia (n)	**fear of** writing
hemophobia (n)	**fear of** blood
hydrophobia (n)	**fear of** water
ornithophobia (n)	**fear of** birds
photophobia (n)	**fear of** light
xenophobia (n)	**fear of** strangers or foreigners
zoophobia (n)	**fear of** animals

Prefixes and Suffixes © 2004 Creative Teaching Press

Vocabulary Sort: -phobia

zoophobia	**fear of** water
hydrophobia	**fear of** light
graphophobia	**fear of** cats
arachnophobia	**fear of** birds
acrophobia	**fear of** blood
ailurophobia	**fear of** strangers or foreigners
hemophobia	**fear of** writing
ornithophobia	**fear of** heights
xenophobia	**fear of** spiders
photophobia	**fear of** animals

Prefixes and Suffixes © 2004 Creative Teaching Press

Read-Around Review: -phobia

I have the first card.
Who has the word that means the **fear of** water?

I have the word **hydrophobia.**
Who has the word that means the **fear of** light?

I have the word **photophobia.**
Who has the word that means the **fear of** birds?

I have the word **ornithophobia.**
Who has the word that means the **fear of** strangers?

I have the word **xenophobia.**
Who has the word that means the **fear of** blood?

I have the word **hemophobia.**
Who has the word that means the **fear of** heights?

I have the word **acrophobia.**
Who has the word that means the **fear of** writing?

I have the word **graphophobia.**
Who has the suffix that means **fear of?**

I have the suffix **-phobia.**
Who has the word that means the **fear of** animals?

I have the word **zoophobia.**
Who has the word that means the **fear of** cats?

I have the word **ailurophobia.**
Who has the word that means the **fear of** spiders?

I have the word **arachnophobia.**
Who has the first card?

Prefixes and Suffixes © 2004 Creative Teaching Press

Name _____   Date _____

Vocabulary Quiz: -phobia

Shade in the bubble for the correct word.

Ⓐ Ⓑ Ⓒ Ⓓ   **1.** Ferdos saw a spider and started screaming. What does she have?
            A) ailurophobia   **B)** arachnophobia   **C)** zoophobia   **D)** spiderphobia

Ⓐ Ⓑ Ⓒ Ⓓ   **2.** Sometimes it seems like nocturnal animals suffer from this fear.
            A) hydrophobia   **B)** ailurophobia   **C)** zoophobia   **D)** photophobia

Ⓐ Ⓑ Ⓒ Ⓓ   **3.** Since Maya was a baby, she has always started crying at the sight of a bird. What fear does
            she suffer from?
            A) ornithophobia   **B)** ailurophobia   **C)** hemophobia   **D)** zoophobia

Ⓐ Ⓑ Ⓒ Ⓓ   **4.** Whenever Nico went into a room full of people he started to panic. His mother wondered
            if he was afraid of all the people he saw and didn't know. She thought he might have
            which fear?
            A) zoophobia   **B)** ailurophobia   **C)** hemophobia   **D)** xenophobia

Ⓐ Ⓑ Ⓒ Ⓓ   **5.** Cindi lives by the ocean, but she won't go in the water. Which fear might she have?
            A) graphophobia   **B)** hemophobia   **C)** hydrophobia   **D)** zoophobia

Ⓐ Ⓑ Ⓒ Ⓓ   **6.** This is a very common fear. Many people have a fear of standing at the top of a high
            building and looking over the side. Which fear is it?
            A) xenophobia   **B)** hemophobia   **C)** acrophobia   **D)** speechophobia

Ⓐ Ⓑ Ⓒ Ⓓ   **7.** Leslie loves dogs and guinea pigs, but she is terrified of cats. What does she suffer from?
            A) ailurophobia   **B)** arachnophobia   **C)** zoophobia   **D)** hydrophobia

Ⓐ Ⓑ Ⓒ Ⓓ   **8.** This is an uncommon fear, especially since every student must do it every day.
            A) graphophobia   **B)** zoophobia   **C)** photophobia   **D)** hydrophobia

Ⓐ Ⓑ Ⓒ Ⓓ   **9.** What does the suffix **-phobia** mean?
            A) around   **B)** a person who   **C)** love of   **D)** fear of

Ⓐ Ⓑ Ⓒ Ⓓ   **10.** A person could not become a doctor with this fear.
            A) ailurophobia   **B)** graphophobia   **C)** hemophobia   **D)** zoophobia

Finish each analogy.

11. ornithophobia : birds :: _____ : cats

12. photophobia : light :: hemophobia : _____

13. writing : _____ :: talking to strangers : xenophobia

14. spiders : arachnophobia :: _____ : hydrophobia

15. bird watcher : ornithophobia :: scuba diver : _____

Prefixes and Suffixes © 2004 Creative Teaching Press

Name _____   Date _____

Review Test: -ology and -phobia

Shade in the bubble for the correct word.

Ⓐ Ⓑ Ⓒ Ⓓ   **1.** A person who studies geology would have a hard time if he or she had a fear of which objects?
        A) rocks   **B)** towers   **C)** airplanes   **D)** wires

Ⓐ Ⓑ Ⓒ Ⓓ   **2.** People who donate money to the animal shelter probably took at least one class in which area of study?
        A) xenophobia   **B)** geology   **C)** zoology   **D)** graphology

Ⓐ Ⓑ Ⓒ Ⓓ   **3.** Dr. Earth would be a great name for someone who studied what?
        A) ecology   **B)** psychology   **C)** sociology   **D)** graphology

Ⓐ Ⓑ Ⓒ Ⓓ   **4.** Lizzie still doesn't want to learn how to swim. She cries in the bathtub. She even refuses to go into the lake. What does she have?
        A) xenophobia   **B)** hemophobia   **C)** hydrophobia   **D)** ornithophobia

Ⓐ Ⓑ Ⓒ Ⓓ   **5.** A nurse in the cardiology department will have a very hard time if she suffers from which fear?
        A) hydrophobia   **B)** hemophobia   **C)** glossophobia   **D)** arachnophobia

Ⓐ Ⓑ Ⓒ Ⓓ   **6.** Of the following fears, which is likely to be the most common?
        A) photophobia   **B)** graphophobia   **C)** arachnophobia   **D)** zoophobia

Ⓐ Ⓑ Ⓒ Ⓓ   **7.** Someone who wants to study sociology will have a hard time if he or she suffers from which of the following fears?
        A) hemophobia   **B)** hydrophobia   **C)** arachnophobia   **D)** xenophobia

Ⓐ Ⓑ Ⓒ Ⓓ   **8.** Anyone who wants to become President of the United States needs to overcome which of the following fears first?
        A) ailurophobia   **B)** glossophobia   **C)** ornithophobia   **D)** arachnophobia

Ⓐ Ⓑ Ⓒ Ⓓ   **9.** If you are interested in learning about how the mind works, which area will you study?
        A) graphology   **B)** bodyology   **C)** psychology   **D)** zoology

Ⓐ Ⓑ Ⓒ Ⓓ   **10.** What does the suffix **-ology** mean?
        A) study of   **B)** fear of   **C)** love of   **D)** after

Ⓐ Ⓑ Ⓒ Ⓓ   **11.** What does the suffix **-phobia** mean?
        A) study of   **B)** fear of   **C)** love of   **D)** after

Ⓐ Ⓑ Ⓒ Ⓓ   **12.** What does **derma** mean in the word *dermatology*?
        A) bones   **B)** skin   **C)** teeth   **D)** heart

Ⓐ Ⓑ Ⓒ Ⓓ   **13.** What does **glosso** most likely relate to in the word *glossophobia*?
        A) speaking   **B)** helping   **C)** shiny   **D)** lips

Ⓐ Ⓑ Ⓒ Ⓓ   **14.** What does **graph** most likely mean in the words *graphology* and *graphophobia*?
        A) math   **B)** science   **C)** history   **D)** writing

Ⓐ Ⓑ Ⓒ Ⓓ   **15.** Which is known as the study of living things?
        A) anthropology   **B)** biology   **C)** geology   **D)** zoology

Word List: -ian, -or

-ian, -or	a person who

Vocabulary	Definitions
centenarian (n)	**a person who** is at least 100 years old
dictator (n)	**a person who** tells people what to do without giving them choices
governor (n)	**a person who** manages the political actions of a state; a state leader
inventor (n)	**a person who** creates something that has never before been created
juror (n)	**a person who** is a member of a jury that listens to both sides of a law case in a courtroom to decide if the defendant is guilty or innocent
legislator (n)	**a person who** makes laws
librarian (n)	**a person who** works in a library
octogenarian (n)	**a person who** is between 80 and 90 years old
translator (n)	**a person who** changes one language into another; **a person who** "cuts across" the language barrier
veterinarian (n)	**a person who** is a doctor of animal science

Prefixes and Suffixes © 2004 Creative Teaching Press

Vocabulary Sort: -ian, -or

dictator	**a person who** creates something that has never before been created
veterinarian	**a person who** manages the political actions of a state; a state leader
legislator	**a person who** works in a library
juror	**a person who** tells people what to do without giving them choices
translator	**a person who** is between 80 and 90 years old
centenarian	**a person who** changes one language into another; **a person who** "cuts across" the language barrier
governor	**a person who** is a member of a jury that listens to both sides of a law case in a courtroom to decide if the defendant is guilty or innocent
librarian	**a person who** is a doctor of animal science
octogenarian	**a person who** is at least 100 years old
inventor	**a person who** makes laws

Read-Around Review: -ian, -or

I have the first card.
Who has the word that names **the person who** makes the laws in your state?

I have the word **legislator.**
Who has the word that names **the person who** works in a library?

I have the word **librarian.**
Who has the word that names **the person who** rules a country or area by
force without giving the people in that area or country any choices?

I have the word **dictator.**
Who has the word that names **the person who** can change one language into another?

I have the word **translator.**
Who has the word that names **the person who** is a doctor
for animals and could take care of your sick pet?

I have the word **veterinarian.**
Who has the word that names **the person who** has made it to her 102nd birthday?

I have the word **centenarian.**
Who has the word that names **the person who** built the very first computer?

I have the word **inventor.**
Who has the word that names **the person who** helps decide
another person's guilt or innocence in a courtroom?

I have the word **juror.**
Who has the word that names **the person who** is between 80 and 90 years old?

I have the word **octogenarian.**
Who has the suffixes that mean **a person who?**

I have the suffixes **-ian** and **-or.**
Who has the word that names **the person who** is a state
leader in charge of giving money to schools?

I have the word **governor.**
Who has the first card?

Name _____   Date _____

Vocabulary Quiz: -ian, -or

Shade in the bubble for the correct word.

Ⓐ Ⓑ Ⓒ Ⓓ   **1.** In history, this person who rules by force and power has not been viewed as a fair leader, since the people in the land have no choices.
A) dictator   **B)** governor   **C)** librarian   **D)** legislator

Ⓐ Ⓑ Ⓒ Ⓓ   **2.** This person sat in a courtroom for three days to listen to the lawyers state their cases. The person helped decide the future of another person.
A) dictator   **B)** librarian   **C)** juror   **D)** translator

Ⓐ Ⓑ Ⓒ Ⓓ   **3.** This person may save the life of one of your pets one day.
A) veterinarian   **B)** translator   **C)** juror   **D)** centenarian

Ⓐ Ⓑ Ⓒ Ⓓ   **4.** What would you call a person who helps you understand what a French person is trying to tell you while visiting Paris, France?
A) veterinarian   **B)** legislator   **C)** governor   **D)** translator

Ⓐ Ⓑ Ⓒ Ⓓ   **5.** This is the person who can help you find books for a report at the library.
A) librarian   **B)** veterinarian   **C)** inventor   **D)** legislator

Ⓐ Ⓑ Ⓒ Ⓓ   **6.** Granny Gums is 88 years old. She'll only be one of these for two more years.
A) centenarian   **B)** librarian   **C)** octogenarian   **D)** governor

Ⓐ Ⓑ Ⓒ Ⓓ   **7.** Someday you could be one of these if you believe that "anything is possible" and you like to create things.
A) legislator   **B)** inventor   **C)** translator   **D)** centenarian

Ⓐ Ⓑ Ⓒ Ⓓ   **8.** If you like to be in charge, perhaps one day you will be one of these.
A) translator   **B)** librarian   **C)** centenarian   **D)** governor

Ⓐ Ⓑ Ⓒ Ⓓ   **9.** Do you like to make rules? Rules are like laws. Perhaps one day you will be one of these.
A) veterinarian   **B)** legislator   **C)** octogenarian   **D)** translator

Ⓐ Ⓑ Ⓒ Ⓓ   **10.** Some news channels put the birthday pictures of these special people on television to help them celebrate their 100th birthdays.
A) octogenarian   **B)** legislators   **C)** veterinarians   **D)** centenarians

Finish each analogy.

11. octogenarian : 80 :: _____ : 100

12. teacher : rules :: _____ : laws

13. doctor : humans :: veterinarian : _____

14. librarian : _____ :: translator : languages

15. juror : listens :: _____ : designs

Prefixes and Suffixes © 2004 Creative Teaching Press

Word List: -ance, -ence

-ance, -ence   state or quality of

Vocabulary	Definitions
annoyance (n)	**the state of being** annoyed; a thing or person who irritates
convenience (n)	**the quality of being** convenient; handy; fits into one's time schedule
defiance (n)	**the state of being** defiant; **the act of** boldly resisting authority; breaking the rules
diligence (n)	**the state of being** diligent; not rushing through a task; taking one's time to do the best work; careful and complete in work
dominance (n)	**the act of being** dominant; **the state of being** in control
elegance (n)	**the state of being** elegant; **the state of showing** richness or grace in style and manners
patience (n)	**the state of being** patient; waiting without any complaint
perseverance (n)	**the state of being** patient in effort; continuous attempts; never giving up
radiance (n)	**the quality or state of being** radiant; brightness
tolerance (n)	**the act of being** tolerant; accepting differences between and among people

Prefixes and Suffixes © 2004 Creative Teaching Press

Vocabulary Sort: -ance, -ence

diligence	**the act of being** tolerant; accepting differences between and among people
perseverance	**the state of being** annoyed; a thing or person that irritates
elegance	**the act of being** dominant; **the state of being** in control
radiance	**the state of being** patient; waiting without any complaint
annoyance	**the quality of being** convenient; handy; fits into one's time schedule
convenience	**the quality or state of being** radiant; brightness
tolerance	**the state of being** defiant; **the act of** boldly resisting authority; breaking the rules
dominance	**the state of being** diligent; not rushing through a task; taking one's time to do the best work; careful and complete in work
defiance	**the state of being** elegant; **the state of showing** richness or grace in style and manners
patience	**the state of being** patient in effort; continuous attempts; never giving up

Prefixes and Suffixes © 2004 Creative Teaching Press

Read-Around Review: -ance, -ence

I have the first card.
Who has the word that describes what someone shows when he or she waits a long time for a turn without ever complaining?

I have the word **patience.**
Who has the word that describes what someone shows when he or she has been bothered by someone or something?

I have the word **annoyance.**
Who has the word that describes what someone shows when he or she rudely refuses to follow the rules?

I have the word **defiance.**
Who has the word that describes what someone shows when he or she seems to shine or glow with happiness?

I have the word **radiance.**
Who has the word that describes what you might show when you have to sit next to someone you really don't like, but you are kind to them anyway?

I have the word **tolerance.**
Who has the word that describes what a person shows when he or she keeps on trying and never gives up?

I have the word **perseverance.**
Who has the word that describes what someone is showing when he or she feels in control and can tell you what to do?

I have the word **dominance.**
Who has the word that describes what someone shows when she looks fancy and well-groomed?

I have the word **elegance.**
Who has the word that describes what you show when you are carefully doing your work to the best of your ability?

I have the word **diligence.**
Who has the suffixes that mean the **state or quality of?**

I have the suffixes **-ance** and **-ence.**
Who has the word that describes something that is handy and easy to use?

I have the word **convenience.**
Who has the first card?

Prefixes and Suffixes © 2004 Creative Teaching Press

Name _____   Date _____

Vocabulary Quiz: -ance, -ence

Shade in the bubble for the correct word.

Ⓐ Ⓑ Ⓒ Ⓓ   **1.** When you can't figure out the answer to the math problem but you keep on trying, what are you showing?
   A) perseverance   **B)** patience   **C)** tolerance   **D)** annoyance

Ⓐ Ⓑ Ⓒ Ⓓ   **2.** David's mom is late picking him up from karate class. Instead of getting mad, he reads his book. What did David show?
   A) elegance   **B)** diligence   **C)** patience   **D)** perseverance

Ⓐ Ⓑ Ⓒ Ⓓ   **3.** Jackie asked Leon if he could help her pull the weeds whenever he had the time. Leon will help pull weeds at his _____.
   A) convenience   **B)** diligence   **C)** perseverance   **D)** defiance

Ⓐ Ⓑ Ⓒ Ⓓ   **4.** Brianna has rewritten her essay three times. She wants to make it her best work. What does Brianna show she has?
   A) perseverance   **B)** diligence   **C)** dominance   **D)** annoyance

Ⓐ Ⓑ Ⓒ Ⓓ   **5.** Every time Jackson holds his baby sister, Esther, she pulls his hair. Jackson thinks this is a bit of an _____.
   A) annoyance   **B)** elegance   **C)** tolerance   **D)** defiance

Ⓐ Ⓑ Ⓒ Ⓓ   **6.** Lucas is constantly getting sent to the principal's office. What must he be showing in his classroom?
   A) diligence   **B)** perseverance   **C)** defiance   **D)** tolerance

Ⓐ Ⓑ Ⓒ Ⓓ   **7.** The bride at the wedding looked amazing. What did she display?
   A) elegance   **B)** patience   **C)** annoyance   **D)** tolerance

Ⓐ Ⓑ Ⓒ Ⓓ   **8.** Roxy, the German Shepherd, usually has _____ over Minnie, the little poodle, because he is bigger.
   A) dominance   **B)** defiance   **C)** radiance   **D)** patience

Ⓐ Ⓑ Ⓒ Ⓓ   **9.** What does the suffix **-ance** mean?
   A) state or quality of   **B)** a person who
   C) in the direction of   **D)** study of

Ⓐ Ⓑ Ⓒ Ⓓ   **10.** Trisha is a vegetarian. At steak restaurants, she must show _____ toward people who enjoy eating meat.
   A) tolerance   **B)** defiance   **C)** perseverance   **D)** diligence

Write the correct word on the line so the sentence makes sense.

11. The prom dress made the girl shine with _____.

12. An important character trait is _____, so that everyone in the world can get along.

13. Keep trying! Don't give up! You can do it! What do these sayings support? _____

14. Successful students show _____ in all of their school work.

15. You won't always get to go first, so having the character trait of _____ is important.

Prefixes and Suffixes © 2004 Creative Teaching Press

Review Test: -ian, -or and -ance, -ence

Shade in the bubble for the correct word.

Ⓐ Ⓑ Ⓒ Ⓓ **1.** Mr. Lopez just invented a homework machine that corrects your homework for you in three seconds! What is Mr. Lopez?
A) legislator **B)** veterinarian **C)** governor **D)** inventor

Ⓐ Ⓑ Ⓒ Ⓓ **2.** Lulu, Garrett's pet iguana, is not looking healthy. Who will Lulu go see?
A) translator **B)** veterinarian **C)** librarian **D)** centenarian

Ⓐ Ⓑ Ⓒ Ⓓ **3.** These people in your state help create the laws that the citizens must follow. Who are they?
A) legislators **B)** dictators **C)** translators **D)** librarians

Ⓐ Ⓑ Ⓒ Ⓓ **4.** Kendra wants to be one of these people when she grows up, so she is learning sign language.
A) dictator **B)** governor **C)** librarian **D)** translator

Ⓐ Ⓑ Ⓒ Ⓓ **5.** Tom is working on fixing his car. Every time he thinks the engine is working, his car stalls two days later. He won't give up, so he's in his garage right now trying to figure out the problem. What does Tom show?
A) perseverance **B)** annoyance **C)** elegance **D)** tolerance

Ⓐ Ⓑ Ⓒ Ⓓ **6.** At the symphony, everyone displays such _____ by dressing up and using good manners.
A) perseverance **B)** diligence **C)** defiance **D)** elegance

Ⓐ Ⓑ Ⓒ Ⓓ **7.** This is a bad trait which will usually get people in trouble.
A) diligence **B)** perseverance **C)** defiance **D)** tolerance

Ⓐ Ⓑ Ⓒ Ⓓ **8.** Something that bothers you a great deal could be described as an _____.
A) annoyance **B)** tolerance **C)** convenience **D)** diligence

Ⓐ Ⓑ Ⓒ Ⓓ **9.** Rhonda's grandma just turned 89. What is she?
A) centenarian **B)** octogenarian **C)** diligent **D)** governor

Ⓐ Ⓑ Ⓒ Ⓓ **10.** What does the suffix **-ian** mean?
A) the study of **B)** a person who **C)** toward **D)** having the quality of

Ⓐ Ⓑ Ⓒ Ⓓ **11.** What does the suffix **-ance** mean?
A) study of **B)** a person who **C)** toward **D)** state or quality of

Ⓐ Ⓑ Ⓒ Ⓓ **12.** What does **octo** mean in the word *octogenarian*?
A) hundred **B)** sixty **C)** seventy **D)** eighty

Ⓐ Ⓑ Ⓒ Ⓓ **13.** What does **contra** most likely relate to in the word *contrarian*?
A) opposite **B)** together **C)** friendly **D)** choice

Ⓐ Ⓑ Ⓒ Ⓓ **14.** What does **dict** most likely mean in the word *dictator*?
A) laws **B)** a person who **C)** tell, say **D)** health

Ⓐ Ⓑ Ⓒ Ⓓ **15.** In order for everyone in the world to get along, what does the world need more of?
A) legislators **B)** dictators **C)** tolerance **D)** defiance

Answer Key

Page 10
1. b
2. c
3. a
4. d
5. c
6. a
7. c
8. b
9. a
10. b
11. predict
12. preceded
13. prevent
14. pretest
15. prejudge

Page 14
1. b
2. a
3. b
4. b
5. c
6. a
7. d
8. c
9. a
10. a
11. postpone
12. postproduction
13. postscript
14. postmark
15. postdate

Page 15
1. c
2. a
3. c
4. a
5. b
6. a
7. a
8. b
9. c
10. b
11. d
12. b
13. b
14. d
15. b

Page 19
1. b
2. d
3. a
4. b
5. c
6. b
7. a
8. d
9. b
10. a
11. monolingual
12. monotone
13. monologue
14. monorail
15. monopoly

Page 23
1. b
2. c
3. a
4. a
5. d
6. b
7. d
8. a
9. b
10. a
11. polygon
12 polysyllabic
13. polydactyl
14. polychromatic
15. polyglot

Page 24
1. a
2. a
3. b
4. b
5. d
6. a
7. c
8. b
9. d
10. b
11. a
12. c
13. d
14. b
15. a

Page 28
1. d
2. b
3. d
4. a
5. a
6. d
7. b
8. b
9. b
10. a
11. unicycle
12. unison
13. unique
14. unicorns
15. unidirectional

Page 32
1. b
2. d
3. c
4. c
5. a
6. a
7. c
8. c
9. b
10. d
11. bifocals
12. bilingual
13. bimonthly
14. biennial
15. bipeds

Page 33
1. c
2. b
3. a
4. b
5. d
6. a
7. b
8. d
9. a
10. c
11. a
12. b
13. b
14. d
15. a

Page 37
1. b
2. a
3. a
4. c
5. a
6. a
7. b
8. c
9. a
10. d
11. tripod
12. trisect
13. triathlon
14. tricycle
15. trilogy

Page 41
1. b
2. a
3. d
4. b
5. d
6. c
7. a
8. c
9. c
10. b
11. quadrilingual
12. quadrennial
13. quadrilateral
14. quadruple
15. quadrisect

Page 42
1. c
2. b
3. b
4. c
5. c
6. b
7. d
8. b
9. c
10. b
11. d
12. c
13. d
14. b
15. c

Page 46
1. c
2. d
3. a
4. b
5. b
6. b
7. d
8. b
9. c
10. d
11. committee
12. coexist
13. commiserate
14. compare
15. community

Page 50
1. d
2. a
3. c
4. d
5. c
6. a
7. c
8. a
9. a
10. a
11. contrary
12. counterfeit
14. contradict
14. counterintuitive
15. contraband

Page 51
1. c
2. b
3. c
4. d
5. d
6. a
7. c
8. b
9. c
10. c
11. b
12. a
13. c
14. b
15. c

Answer Key

Page 55
1. b
2. d
3. c
4. c
5. a
6. b
7. b
8. a
9. b
10. a
11. subordinate
12. subfreezing
13. submerge
14. subway
15. subcutaneous

Page 59
1. b
2. b
3. b
4. a
5. b
6. d
7. d
8. c
9. a
10. d
11. surplus
12. supervisor
13. superb
14. surreal
15. surprise

Page 60
1. c
2. b
3. c
4. a
5. b
6. c
7. d
8. c
9. c
10. c
11. a
12. b
13. a
14. a
15. d

Page 64
1. b
2. a
3. b
4. a
5. d
6. b
7. d
8. a
9. c
10. b
11. untidy
12. unworthy
13. unconscious
14. unmistakable
15. unnecessary

Page 68
1. d
2. b
3. a
4. b
5. a
6. d
7. a
8. d
9. b
10. a
11. discontinue
12. dismal
13. disrespectful
14. disobedient
15. disadvantage

Page 69
1. d
2. a
3. a
4. b
5. b
6. c
7. c
8. d
9. a
10. b
11. b
12. b
13. a
14. d
15. d

Page 73
1. b
2. a
3. c
4. a
5. c
6. c
7. a
8. a
9. a
10. b
11. interrupted
12. interactive
13. interpreter
14. Internet
15. intermission

Page 77
1. d
2. b
3. a
4. b
5. a
6. a
7. b
8. b
9. b
10. d
11. intranasal
12. intradermal
13. sports between schools
14. intravenous
15. intrastate

Page 78
1. b
2. d
3. a
4. c
5. a
6. b
7. d
8. a
9. a
10. c
11. d
12. b
13. c
14. a
15. a

Page 82
1. d
2. b
3. a
4. c
5. d
6. a
7. c
8. c
9. b
10. c
11. circumference
12. circumvent
13. fly around the U.S.
14. (answers will vary)
15. cir-cum-flex

Page 86
1. c
2. a
3. d
4. b
5. c
6. a
7. c
8. d
9. c
10. b
11. translucent
12. transfer
13. travel across a continent
14. (answers will vary)
15. trans-la-tion

Page 87
1. d
2. a
3. d
4. b
5. d
6. b
7. a
8. c
9. a
10. a
11. a
12. b
13. c
14. b
15. c

Page 91
1. c
2. d
3. b
4. a
5. b
6. d
7. b
8. a
9. b
10. c
11. malignant
12. malnutrition
13. malodorous
14. (answers will vary)
15. malfunction

Page 95
1. a
2. c
3. a
4. a
5. a
6. b
7. b
8. c
9. a
10. a
11. mistreat
12. misunderstand
13. mistake
14. mischievous
15. luck

Page 96
1. d
2. b
3. d
4. b
5. c
6. d
7. b
8. a
9. a
10. a
11. a
12. c
13. b
14. b
15. a

Answer Key

Page 100
1. b
2. d
3. d
4. a
5. d
6. a
7. b
8. a
9. a
10. a
11. reelected
12. refund
13. recheck
14. reclosable
15. respond

Page 104
1. d
2. a
3. b
4. a
5. b
6. d
7. c
8. b
9. a
10. a
11. symmetry
12. symposium
13. sympathy
14. synonyms
15. synthetic

Page 105
1. c
2. a
3. a
4. d
5. a
6. a
7. c
8. b
9. b
10. a
11. a
12. d
13. b
14. b
15. b

Page 109
1. d
2. a
3. b
4. d
5. c
6. b
7. c
8. b
9. a
10. c
11. hypothesis
12. hypothermia
13. hypodermic
14. hypoglycemia
15. hy-po-ten-sion

Page 113
1. b
2. c
3. a
4. c
5. b
6. a
7. b
8. b
9. a
10. c
11. hyperthermia
12. hypersensitive
13. hypercritical
14. hyperbole
15. hyperactive

Page 114
1. a
2. d
3. d
4. d
5. b
6. a
7. a
8. c
9. b
10. a
11. b
12. a
13. b
14. d
15. b

Page 118
1. b
2. c
3. a
4. d
5. b
6. b
7. b
8. d
9. a
10. c
11. detachable
12. acceptable
13. repairable
14. washable
15. portable

Page 122
1. a
2. d
3. a
4. c
5. b
6. c
7. a
8. c
9. d
10. a
11. odorless
12. fearless
13. speechless
14. tireless
15. worthless

Page 123
1. b
2. a
3. d
4. b
5. c
6. b
7. c
8. c
9. b
10. a
11. d
12. c
13. a
14. c
15. d

Page 127
1. a
2. a
3. a
4. d
5. d
6. a
7. a
8. b
9. a
10. c
11. ecology
12. animals
13. dermatology
14. psychology
15. geology

Page 131
1. b
2. d
3. a
4. d
5. c
6. c
7. a
8. a
9. d
10. c
11. ailurophobia
12. blood
13. graphophobia
14. water
15. hydrophobia

Page 132
1. a
2. c
3. a
4. c
5. b
6. c
7. d
8. b
9. c
10. a
11. b
12. b
13. a
14. d
15. b

Page 136
1. a
2. c
3. a
4. d
5. a
6. c
7. b
8. d
9. b
10. d
11. centenarian
12. legislator
13. animals
14. books
15. inventor

Page 140
1. a
2. c
3. a
4. b
5. a
6. c
7. a
8. a
9. a
10. a
11. radiance
12. tolerance
13. perseverance
14. diligence
15. patience

Page 141
1. d
2. b
3. a
4. d
5. a
6. d
7. c
8. a
9. b
10. b
11. d
12. d
13. a
14. c
15. c